THE WHISKY AND GIN LOVER'S GUIDE TO SCOTLAND

THE WHISKY AND GIN LOVER'S GUIDE TO

SCOTLAND

ANGELA YOUNGMAN

AN IMPRINT OF PEN & SWORD BOOKS LTD.
YORKSHIRE – PHILADELPHIA

First published in Great Britain in 2025
White Owl
An imprint of
Pen & Sword Books Ltd
Yorkshire – Philadelphia

Copyright © Angela Youngman, 2025

ISBN 978 1 03611 776 4

The right of Angela Youngman to be identified as Author of this work has been asserted by her in accordance with the Copyright, Designs and Patents Act 1988.

A CIP catalogue record for this book is available from the British Library.

All rights reserved. No part of this book may be reproduced, transmitted, downloaded, decompiled or reverse engineered in any form or by any means, electronic or mechanical including photocopying, recording or by any information storage and retrieval system, without permission from the Publisher in writing. NO AI TRAINING: Without in any way limiting the Author's and Publisher's exclusive rights under copyright, any use of this publication to "train" generative artificial intelligence (AI) technologies to generate text is expressly prohibited. The Author and Publisher reserve all rights to license uses of this work for generative AI training and development of machine learning language models.

Design: SJmagic DESIGN SERVICES, India.

The Publisher's authorised representative in the EU for product safety is Authorised Rep Compliance Ltd., Ground Floor, 71 Lower Baggot Street, Dublin D02 P593, Ireland.
www.arccompliance.com

For a complete list of Pen & Sword titles please contact

PEN & SWORD BOOKS LIMITED
George House, Beevor Street, Off Pontefract Road, Hoyle Mill, Barnsley, South Yorkshire, England, S71 1HN.
E-mail: enquiries@pen-and-sword.co.uk
Website: www.pen-and-sword.co.uk

or

PEN AND SWORD BOOKS
1950 Lawrence Road, Havertown, PA 19083, USA
E-mail: uspen-and-sword@casematepublishers.com
Website: www.penandswordbooks.com

FSC
www.fsc.org
MIX
Paper | Supporting responsible forestry
FSC™ C016779

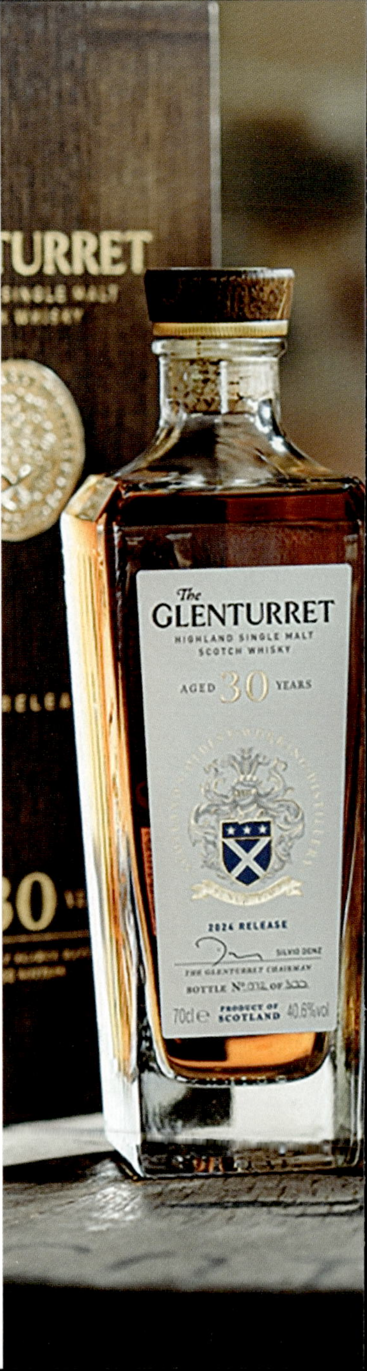

The
GLENTURRET
HIGHLAND SINGLE MALT
SCOTCH WHISKY
AGED 25 YEARS
2024 RELEASE
70cl
PRODUCT OF
SCOTLAND
41%vol

CONTENTS

1

WHISKY

Think of Scotland, and you immediately think of beautiful scenery, pipers, tartan and whisky. This amber-coloured nectar has been distilled in Scotland for centuries, and is an integral part of the country's heritage and culture. In fact, it is Scotland's national drink, and its biggest export. Gin is almost equally well known as an iconic Scottish beverage. Scotland produces over 70% of the gin sold in the UK.

With over 240 whisky and gin distilleries located across the country, a distillery visit forms an essential part of any stay in Scotland, especially since many of the distilleries offer both gin and whisky on the same site. It is the perfect way to discover what makes

▾ ***Piper playing the bagpipes outside the Kingsbarns distillery.*** (© Kingsbarns)

Scottish whisky and gin so special. These are alcoholic beverages that have become iconic, creating legends, inspiring literature and films and having a major impact on medicine and even world history.

Thousands of visitors every year set out to explore the delights of the Scotch whisky and gin distilleries located in the various regions that now comprise the whisky landscape of Scotland. This is because the exact location of a distillery determines the resultant flavour of the spirits, since everything from the water source to the presence of peat in the soil can affect the taste. These are regions that have developed over the past couple of hundred years as a way of instantly identifying key whisky characteristics – characteristics that are frequently shared with gin production. Exploring this unique heritage amid the beauty of the Scottish scenery and Scotland's historic towns and cities makes for some entertaining, memorable journeys.

WHISKY OR WHISKEY?

The spelling of this alcoholic drink depends greatly on where you live. The most common spelling is *whisky*. This is how it is spelt in Scotland, England, Wales, Canada, Japan and most other countries worldwide. In Ireland and the USA, the preferred spelling is *whiskey*. Whatever the spelling, the base spirit and concept are always the same – what varies is the style and flavours.

▼ ***Aerial view of the Scottish countryside from the Nc'nean distillery towards the Isle of Mull.*** (© Nc'nean)

WHAT IS WHISKY?

Whisky is distilled from fermented cereal grain, water and yeast before being aged in wooden casks. If it is labelled 'Scotch whisky', then by law it has to be made in Scotland. There are different types of whisky depending on the grain, malt and blends. According to the Scotch Whisky Association, nine out of ten bottles of Scotch whisky are blended versions, combining both single grain and single malt whisky. A blend may contain up to sixty different Scotch whiskies.

TYPES OF WHISKY

According to the Scotch Whisky Association there are four types of Scotch whisky.

1. **Single malt**. This type of whisky has been distilled at just one distillery using water and barley. No other cereals have been used in its production. Distillation has taken place in a copper pot still, and all bottling takes place in Scotland.
2. **Blended malt**. This type of whisky comprises a mixture of single malt

▾ ***Benriach whisky barrels maturing in the warehouse.*** (© Benriach)

Scotch whiskies that have been distilled at one or more distilleries.

3 **Single grain**. This is whisky that has been distilled at a single distillery from water and malted barley, with or without the whole grains, malted or unmalted, of other cereals.
4 **Blended grain**. This is a blend of various single grain Scotch whiskies. They may have come from one or more distilleries.

To be described as *blended* Scotch whisky, the whisky must contain one or more single malt Scotch whiskies plus one or more single grain whiskies.

The alcoholic strength of whisky can vary. By law in the UK, all whisky possesses at least 40% alcohol by volume (ABV), while Scotch destined for export often has a minimum alcohol strength of 43% by volume.

For centuries, the *proof* strength of whisky was measured when whisky and gunpowder were mixed and ignited. If the gunpowder flashed, then the whisky was regarded as meeting the required strength. Ignition would not take place if the whisky was not strong enough. During the nineteenth century the Sikes hydrometer offered a more accurate solution. This continued to be used until 1980 when Britain, along with most other countries, adopted a measurement system recommended by the International Organization of Legal Metrology. This system measures the strength of alcohol using a *percentage by volume* at 20°C.

WHISKY DISTILLERY REGIONS

The Scotch Whisky Association divides whisky production into five separate regions: *Campbeltown*, *Highland*, *Islay*, *Lowland* and *Speyside*. Each region produces a different style of whisky. There can be considerable differences in taste between regions.

Campbeltown

This is the smallest of the Scottish whisky regions. Campbeltown itself lies on the Kintyre peninsula, which is part of the county of Argyll on the western side of Scotland. At one time there were over thirty distilleries in the area. Springbank is the oldest operating distillery in the region, dating back to 1828. Campbeltown whiskies are rich and complex, possessing hints of salt, smoke, fruit, vanilla and toffee. Typical brands include Glen Scotia and Kilkerran.

The first reference to whisky being produced in the Kintyre peninsula was recorded in 1591. It soon became a centre of whisky smuggling and the illegal production of *uisge beatha* – the water of life, also known as whisky. In the nineteenth century, demand for Campbeltown whisky grew rapidly resulting in the town becoming one of the richest in Britain by 1891. Changing taste preferences and recession led to

Scotland's whisky regions as part of an explanatory display at Kingsbarns distillery. (© Kingsbarns)

Heather in bloom at Tomatin. (© Tomatin)

a decrease in whisky producers during the twentieth century.

Highland

The largest of all the Scotch whisky areas, the Highland region includes many of the islands that surround the Scottish coast. It stretches from the west to the east coast, and includes the Shetland and Orkney Islands. Not surprisingly, Highland whisky possesses a vast variety of flavours and characters covering every possible taste including salty, fruity and spicy, often with a flavour of heather. A common denominator is the presence of a peaty taste due to the nature of the soil. Typical brands include Glenmorangie and Glenfiddich.

Islay

An island just twenty-five miles long and fifteen miles wide located off the coast of south-west Scotland, Islay possesses a long established tradition of whisky-making. Bowmore is the oldest of the Islay distilleries, being established in 1779. It produces single malt whisky which is primarily smoky and peaty in style, often possessing hints of salt and seaweed. Typical Islay whiskies include Ardbeg and Laphroaig.

Lowland

Lowland whisky originates from southern Scotland, an area stretching from the Scottish border to just north of Glasgow and Edinburgh, roughly between the Clyde Estuary and the River Tay. Light in character, Lowland whisky tends to be soft and smooth, flavoured with hints of grass, honeysuckle, cream, ginger, toffee, toast and cinnamon. Its characteristic whisky style has resulted in the nickname of 'Lowland Ladies', due to the presence of lighter, sweeter and floral tones. Typical brands include Glenkinchie and Eden Mill.

Speyside

Located on the eastern side of Scotland, Speyside covers an area surrounding the River Spey and stretches from Inverness to Aberdeen. It is home to the largest group of distilleries in Scotland including many of the most well known such as Glenlivit and The Macallan. The oldest distillery is Strathisla which was established in 1786. Usually matured in sherry casks, Speyside whisky tends to have a fruity, peaty taste together with hints of apple, pear, honey, vanilla and spice.

HOW IS WHISKY PRODUCED?

Barley, wheat, rye or corn are the most common grains used in whisky production. In Scotland, wheat or barley are normally used, although rye is beginning to appear. The type of grain will affect the taste of the whisky. The basic concept of distilling whisky has changed little over the years.

The chosen grain first has to be *malted*. This involves being soaked in water-filled tanks and then air dried. The aroma of the materials used in the heating stove, such as peat bricks, heather or seaweed, will affect the flavour of the malted grain. The more smoke produced in the kiln, the smokier will be the end product.

The next stage involves pulverising the malted grains in a milling machine, before being *mashed* in a tank of hot water one or more times, in what is known as the *tun room*. This turns the

◂ ***Milling grain at the Crafty distillery.*** (© Crafty)

▾ ***Stillmen at the Glenturret distillery, 1905.*** (© Glenturret)

The Ardnamurchan tun room.
(© Ardnamurchan)

mash into a sweet liquid known as the *wort*. After passing the wort through a heat exchanger to cool it, the wort enters a fermentation tank and remains there for two or more days.

The next stage involves *distillation* in a *still*. The size and design of still varies considerably. The liquid is heated to boiling point, and the vapours are captured before being condensed back into an alcoholic liquid. This liquid is then *matured* (aged) in barrels for at least three years, during which the colour and flavour of the whisky will develop.

Following this three-year maturation period, the whisky is *finished* by being placed in *casks* that have previously held other beverages such as wine, sherry or bourbon. The length of time the whisky is matured, together with the type of wood, the condition of the interior of the cask and the microclimate in which the casks are stored will affect the taste of the whisky. At this stage the whisky may also be blended with other types of whisky. At the end of the finishing period, the whisky will be bottled and sold. The alcoholic strength can vary, but as noted above, in order to comply with UK legislative requirements, it has to possess a minimum bottling strength of 40% ABV.

▲ ***Barrels containing whisky maturing in the Tomatin warehouse.*** (© Tomatin)

EXPORT OF SCOTCH WHISKY

According to the Scotch Whisky Association, global exports of Scotch whisky topped £5.6 billion in 2023. This was the equivalent of 1.35 billion 70cl bottles of whisky, at a rate of 43 per second. The vast majority of these bottles were exported to the Asia-Pacific region, particularly China, Singapore and Taiwan. Demand for premium Scotch whisky and single malts is especially high. In Europe, France is the largest market for Scotch whisky. The USA is another big market and has been known to import whisky totalling £1 billion or more. The Scotch whisky industry now contributes £7.1 billion to the UK economy as a whole and is one of the biggest Scottish exports.

ANGELS' SHARE

This is a term frequently mentioned during distillery tours. It refers to the way in which small quantities of spirits evaporate during the whisky ageing process, squeezing through the wood and passing into the atmosphere.

Regarded as a sacrifice to the heavens, it is described as the 'Angels' share', and accounts for about 2% of the liquid. Such evaporation is most common in young spirits, especially whisky, and slows down as time progresses.

The size of whisky casks can make a big difference. According to Glenlivet, whiskies stored in smaller casks will experience a higher rate of evaporation simply because there is a much greater wood-to-liquid ratio. Evaporation will never stop, and by the end of the maturation period for a twenty-year-old whisky, around 40% of the overall volume could well have been lost. Even the way the casks are stored affects the size of the angels' share – storing casks on racks or pallets raised slightly from the ground allows air to circulate around them, resulting in greater evaporation. Traditional *dunnage warehouses* such as those at Glenlivet have a gravel floor and smaller numbers of casks, which reduces the rate of evaporation.

In the gin industry, the angels' share is lost into the air during the distillation process.

Only one distiller is known to have ever captured some of the angels' share. This was an English gin distillery based in Cambridge, which utilised innovative scientific techniques involving atmospheric pressure to preserve the angels' share normally lost during distillation. A time consuming process, it took nearly fifty distillations to produce one bottle, known as Watenshi gin, retailing at around £2,800.

MIXERS AND SPIRITS

Although whisky and gin are often drunk neat as a pure spirit, diluting with a mixer is common. Whisky and water is a traditional option, and according to research undertaken at the University of Sweden in 2023, water has a beneficial impact. It seems that water boosts the flavour molecules, bringing out the unique flavour of the whisky. Soda is another favourite mixer, often with some ice and lemon, for a similar reason since it is a flavour enhancer and can reduce any sweetness. Some people even use Coke as a mixer so as to decrease the strength of the drink, but this obviously affects the taste of the whisky.

Tonic water is the usual option for mixing with gin. This tradition goes back to the nineteenth century when British people visiting India frequently suffered from malaria and scurvy on the long voyage. A mixture of quinine, limes and/or lemons provided a cure for both illnesses. This became known as tonic water, which is somewhat bitter to drink. Adding gin, sugar and ice to the tonic water resulted in a palatable beverage. The first tonic water was patented by Erasmus Bond in 1858, and was soon being manufactured in large quantities, particularly for export overseas. The most famous of the tonic water manufacturers was Schweppes, which specialised in carbonated artificial mineral waters and produced a version marketed as 'Indian Tonic Water'. By 1868, a copy of the Anglo-Indian *Oriental Sporting Magazine* referred to people watching a horse race asking for a 'gin and tonic' at the end of the race.

Gin, with a mixer if available, has always been a popular drink. During the Second World War, playwright Noël Coward noted that, 'When the warning sounds, I gather up some pillows, a pack of cards and a bottle of gin, tuck myself beneath the stairs and do very nicely ... until the "all clear" sounds.' Films like *Casablanca* frequently featured people drinking gin while army officers on active service frequently distilled their own version. Serving in France, Major Dennis Thatcher and his officer colleagues made gin by mixing oil pressed from juniper berries into alcohol. According to Thatcher, 'a mouthful of this stuff nearly blew our heads off'. He said it 'tasted like hell' but they drank it anyway, mixing it with fruit juice since there was no tonic water available.

Throughout the twentieth century, Schweppes Indian Tonic Water was the most frequently drunk brand, available in pubs, clubs and other establishments. During the Second World War, production of the Schweppes brand ceased, but drinkers were continuously reminded of its existence with advertisements indicating that Schweppes would return as soon as the war ended. A tagline, 'What you need is Schweppervescence', was created to promote the brand, and this tagline was first used on railway station banners during the 1946 London Victory Parade. Within two years, Schweppes Indian Tonic Water was available for purchase again.

At the beginning of the twenty-first century, Charles Rolls and Tim Warrilow set up a new premium mixers company called Fever-Tree, using high quality botanicals in order to offer an enhanced taste. The brand proved extremely successful and in 2014 Fever-Tree was even operating pop-up bars selling 160 gins from international distilleries. Customers could try different gins and tonic waters in order to identify their favourite combinations.

WHISKY HISTORY

The concept of distilling alcoholic drinks fermented from grain goes back thousands of years. The Bible differentiates beer and wine from 'strong drink', and in ancient Greece the philosopher Aristotle refers to the distillation process. In Scotland, whisky has long been known as *aqua vitae* (the water of life) and as *usquebaugh*.

The first known written Scottish reference to the production of whisky

▲ ***The ruins of Lindores abbey, home of Brother John Cor.*** (© Lindores Abbey)

appears in the Exchequer Roll of King James IV indicating a 'payment made to Brother John Cor by precept of the comptroller, as he asserts, by the King's command, to make *aqua vitae* within the period of the account, 8 bolls of malt'. Recent research indicates that Brother John Cor lived near Falkland Palace in Fife, at the abbey of Lindores, a site much favoured by King James IV. There were many historical links between the abbey and the palace.

The popularity of *aqua vitae* was clearly apparent by 1527. Hector Boece, principal of Aberdeen University, wrote in *The History and Chronicles of Scotland*, that 'when my ancestors were determined to be merie, they used a kind of aqua vitae, void of all spice, and onelie consisting of such herbs and roots as grow in their own gardens'. Typical herbs would have included hyssop, lavender, marjoram, rosemary, wild mountain thyme and heather.

As the years progressed, travellers around Scotland noted the dominance of *aqua vitae* as a drink, often in different strengths. In 1695, Martin

Martin's *Description of the Western Isles of Scotland* noted:

> There plenty of corn was such, as disposed the Natives to brew several sorts of liquors, as common *usquebaugh*, another call'd Trestarig, Aqua-vitae, three times distilled, which is strong and hot; a third sort is four times distilled, and this by the natives is called *usquebaugh-bual* ... which at first taste affects all the members of the Body; two spoonfuls of this Last Liquor is sufficient dose, and if any man exceed this it would presently stop his breath and endanger his life.

Many years later in 1726, Captain Edmund Burt noted that 'Some of the Highland gentlemen are immoderate drinkers of usky; even three or four quarts at a sitting.' There was even a version of punch in which they 'mixed it with water and honey, or with milk and honey: at other times the mixture is only the *aqua vitae*, sugar and butter; they burn till the butter and sugar are dissolved'.

By 1773, when Dr Samuel Johnson and James Boswell toured Scotland, whisky had become part of normal life. Dr Johnson wrote, 'A man of the Hebrides ... as soon as he appears in the morning, swallows a glass of whisky ... They are not a drunken race, but no man is so abstemious as to refuse the morning dram, which they call a *skalk*' (which comes from the Gaelic *sgalic*, a blow to the head).

Taxation invariably created problems for distillers and drinkers, with Scotland being divided into two halves for Excise purposes in 1784. Highland whisky tended to be of higher quality, and was distilled by farmers using their own small stills. Demand for this whisky was high, but officially it could not be exported across the Highland line. Lowland distillers prospered as they were able to export their produce at low prices, often to be turned into gin – a drink that was much in demand in London. Lowland whisky was not held in high esteem. Robert Burns wrote in a letter dated 1788 that 'the whisky of this country [Lowlands] is a most rascally liquor, and by consequence only drunk by the most rascally part of the inhabitants'.

In many areas, whisky production went underground. The production of moonshine became common in many remote locations, and taxes went unpaid. There were hidden distilleries – some under bridges, some in clock towers and even a few hidden in house cellars, enabling steam and smoke to be piped up through the chimney. The clergy were known to hide whisky under their pulpits, and there were occasions when illicit spirits were moved around in coffins. Smuggling was rampant, and disputes between smugglers, distillers, couriers and drinkers were common. By the early nineteenth century, over 14,000 illicit stills were being seized by the Excise every year and it was said that more than half the whisky drunk in Scotland had not involved any tax payments.

Whisky was a normal part of life whether illicit or legal. Elizabeth Grant of Rothiemurchus described life in the 1820s, saying 'Decent gentlemen begin the day with a dram ... In our house, the bottle of whisky, with the accompaniment of a silver salver or small glasses, was placed on the side table with cold meats every morning.' She reported that 'my father sent word to me ... to empty my pet bin, where there was whisky long in wood, long in uncorked bottles, mild as milk, and the true contraband gout in it'.

When George IV visited Edinburgh he admired the whisky on offer, calling for a bottle of what was then illicit Glenlivet whisky.

The sheer scale of smuggling and Excise problems led to the Duke of Gordon (on whose lands illicit whisky was frequently produced) to propose in the House of Lords that whisky should be produced legally. The Highland line was finally scrapped in 1823. Duty payable was halved, and a rebate given if the distillers used 100% malt. As a result, many new distilleries were established, such as The Macallan.

The invention of the columnar patent still (also known as a Coffey still) in 1831 enabled continuous distillation to take place, resulting in the production of grain whisky. All these developments paved the way for

Tales of The Macallan. (© The Macallan)

the foundation of the modern whisky and gin industry. Brands such as The Macallan, Glenturret and Glenfiddich became household names.

The Johnnie Walker image of a striding man, dressed in Georgian style clothing, first appeared in 1820 having been developed by a Kilmarnock grocer named John Walker. This figure starred in the world's first filmed advertisement in 1898, becoming an instantly recognisable image worldwide.

In 2022, the world's oldest Scotch whisky was discovered hidden behind a cellar door in Blair Castle. It was distilled in 1833 and sipped by a young Queen Victoria. Around twenty-four bottles were found at the back of a shelf. The whisky had been bottled in 1841, and rebottled in 1932. Blair Castle research plus carbon dating and authentication of the whisky by the Scottish Universities Environmental Research Centre proved its historic origins. In 2023, the bottles sold at auction for a combined total of £385,360. Individual bottles sold for an average of £16,068.

INSPIRED BY THE DRAM

Throughout history, there have been many stories inspired by whisky and gin. Some may be true, while others may be the result of imbibing a little too much.

Atholl brose

Varying stories exist as to the origins of this liqueur-style drink made by mixing oatmeal, honey and whisky. One legend suggests that the drink dates back to 1475 when the Earl of Atholl suppressed a Highland rebellion by adding Atholl brose to the rebel leader's well. This enabled him to capture a very drunk enemy.

Another version refers to a giant who lived in the land of Atholl (now part of Perthshire) who kept stealing all the grain supplies. A young hunter named Dougal set out to deal with the giant. He discovered the giant's stores of oats, honey and whisky. Dougal poured the oats into the hollow boulder that acted as the giant's drinking cup, before adding the honey and all the whisky. When the giant fell asleep after drinking the mixture, Dougal emerged from his hiding place and slew the giant. Returning to his people as a hero, his recipe for Atholl brose became part of their heritage.

Inspiring Robert Burns

Scottish poet Robert Burns found whisky inspiring. He wrote a poem relating to the passing of the 1784 Act on whisky distillation, and celebrated the role whisky played in ordinary life. He wrote:

I sing the juice Scots bear can mak us
In glass or jug
O thou, my Muse! Guild auld Scotch
Drink
Inspire me, till I lisp and wink
To sing thy name

and that

Freedom and whisky gang thegither,
Tak aff your dram.

Interestingly, he originally trained as an Exciseman hunting down illicit whisky stills and seeking to enforce taxes. He later wrote a poem called 'The Deil's Awa Wi' The Exciseman' reflecting the popular attitude towards the Excise.

The drink fit for a gentleman

Novelist Sir Walter Scott was an enthusiastic whisky drinker both neat and as hot toddies before bedtime, regarding it as the only liquor fit for a gentleman. He is believed to be the first novelist to mention Scotch whisky in his books. In *Waverley* he wrote, 'The allowance of whisky ... would have appeared prodigal to any but Highlanders, who, living entirely in the open air and in a very moist climate, can consume great quantities of ardent spirits without the usual baneful effects either upon the brain or constitution.' During George IV's visit to Edinburgh in 1822, Sir Walter Scott arranged entertainments in which Highland single malt Whisky made a prominent appearance. Glenmorangie distillery adopted the image of Sir Walter as part of its trademark.

Byron's wedding cask

Another famous poet, Lord Byron, celebrated his wedding to Lady Annabella Milbanke with whisky. During the celebrations, he gave a cask of his favourite Spey single malt whisky to King George III. Visitors to Kew Palace, London, can see a replica of that wedding cask.

Smugglers' tales

With high taxes and high demand for whisky and gin, smuggling was all too common in the late eighteenth and early nineteenth centuries, which resulted in numerous legendary encounters between smugglers, local people and the Excisemen.

Between 1796 and 1798, there was a shortage of money in the Shetland Islands because merchants were buying so much smuggled gin. Local accounts indicated that illicit gin had 'drained the poor of this country ... of every shilling they could raise'. It was a very profitable business since a fisherman might only earn the equivalent of 25p per week, which was equal to the duty on a cask of spirits. Buying a barrel of gin for £1 and selling it for £4, then diluting it to a drinkable strength for wider distribution, offered considerable economic benefits.

With so much money at stake, violence was never far away. On 1 December 1798, a battle broke out between Philip Kennedy, a well known gin smuggler, and the Excisemen. Kennedy had just unloaded sixteen ankers of gin at the small port of Cransdale in Aberdeenshire and was taking it inland. The Excisemen lay in wait at the Kirk of Slains. When Kennedy arrived, he was attacked by the Excisemen and a fight broke out during which Kennedy received a sword blow that cleaved his skull open. Local legend has it that he managed to stagger a quarter of mile before collapsing and dying. Kennedy's exploits attracted considerable publicity and novelist Sir Walter Scott incorporated the story into his novel, *Guy Mannering*.

Local accounts show that the Excisemen were often treated roughly. Writing in the nineteenth century, William Alexander noted that the Exciseman was regarded as 'a fit subject for rough handling as occasion offered. To tie his legs together and fasten his hands forcible behind his back and leave him lying helpless on the lone hillside was not deemed out of place by any means'.

Gunsgreen's hidden secrets

Tucked away on Berwickshire's coast is the small town of Eyemouth, once a haven for smuggling. High on the headland is Gunsgreen House, built in the eighteenth century by John Nisbet. By day he was a respected merchant – but at night he was a busy smuggler of tea, gin, brandy and other desirable items. The house is quite unique. Designed by John Adam, one of the most famous architects of the period, it is a smugglers' paradise since it was adapted for Nisbet's 'special requirements'.

Gunsgreen House – a smugglers' paradise.
(Angela Youngman)

▲ ***Hiding place for smuggled goods tucked away in the bookcase.*** (© Gunsgreen House)

▼ ***Hidey-hole outside a bedroom where smugglers hid when customs raided the house.*** (© Gunsgreen House)

Every room in the house, all the corridors, landing and stairs contain unexpected cavities and hidey-holes. Pull up a hidden hatch and find a large space underneath; gently prise open a section of wall to find a metal-lined cavity designed to hold large quantities of tea. Even the fireplace moves to reveal hidden corners.

Whisky and anatomy

During the nineteenth century, the City of Edinburgh allocated 12 gallons of whisky every year to the University's Anatomy Museum. The whisky was intended to preserve anatomical specimens such as organs taken from dissected bodies. The University's School of Medicine was renowned for its dissections including those linked to bodies provided by Burke and Hare, notorious resurrectionists who eventually started murdering to provide fresh cadavers. Since more than one technician involved in the dissections was actually dismissed for being constantly drunk on the job, it is very likely that not all the whisky was used for its intended purpose!

Whisky Galore! and the Second World War

During the Second World War, the *SS Politician* ran aground off the coast of the Hebridean island of Eriskay. It was carrying a cargo of 28,000 cases of malt whisky plus 290,000 10-shilling notes. Much of it disappeared and was not recovered. The incident inspired Compton Mackenzie to write a novel called *Whisky Galore!*, which became a top-ranking comedy film by Ealing Studios. In the film, a small Scottish island is horrified when supplies of whisky run out. Then a freighter, *SS Cabinet Minister*, runs aground with 50,000 cases of whisky, which are gleefully removed by the islanders. Pompous Home Guard commander, Captain Waggett, sets out to regain control of the whisky, only to be opposed by the local people led by shopkeeper Joseph Macroon and his daughters. Filmed entirely on location, *Whisky Galore!* is regarded as one of the best British films of the twentieth century.

Biawa, the distillery ghost

During the Boer War, Colonel Grant of Glenrothes distillery fame rescued an orphan child named Biawa 'Byeway' Makalaga. He took the boy back to Scotland, where he grew up and eventually became involved in whisky production at Glenrothes. He was buried in a grave overlooking the distillery. It seems that he became very fond of the distillery, as after his death his ghost appeared in the still room investigating the installation of a new pair of stills. After investigations by a paranormal expert, it was felt that the stills needed to be moved slightly. It seems that

Byeway believed that the stills had been misaligned and would affect the quality of the spirit. Since then, it has become a distillery tradition to give a 'Toast to the Ghost' with a dram of Glenrothes.

James Bond

Reading Ian Fleming's James Bond novels, it's clear 007 is definitely a whisky drinker. In both *Live and Let Die* and *Moonraker* he drinks Scotch.

Although brands are rarely mentioned, Bond enjoys a whisky and soda. So much so, that in *Thunderball* he wakes up one morning with a headache after drinking eleven whisky sodas the previous night. In *Live and Let Die* he orders scotch and soda – 'Haig & Haig Pinchbottle' – during a meeting with Felix Leiter. Prior to a meeting with Sir Hugo Drax in *Moonraker*, Bond opts for Black & White blended Scotch whisky. Fleming writes: 'He sat at the bar and waited while the man poured two measures of Black & White and put the glass in front him with a syphon of soda. Bond filled the glass with soda and drank.'

This fascination with whisky continued into the iconic Bond films. Pierce Brosnan's Bond opted for a Talisker ten-year-old whisky, and more recently Daniel Craig's Bond chose The Macallan. In *Skyfall*, Bond is seen drinking The Macallan Fine & Rare 1962. Interestingly, The Macallan celebrated its James Bond links with a sixtieth anniversary release in special archive-based Bond-themed packaging and bottles for each anniversary decade.

The Angels' Share

A Ken Loach film made in 2012, *The Angels' Share* is a comedy heist movie based in Scotland. It tells the story of a young man who has just avoided a prison sentence. While attending a community payback group, he and his friends visit a whisky distillery where he discovers a skill in identifying flavours. Later, he becomes involved in attempts to steal a 'priceless' whisky coming up for auction. Glengoyne and Balblair distilleries were used for the exterior shots while Deanston was the setting for the interior scenes.

WHISKY TRADITIONS

Burns Night

Dedicated to the memory of poet Robert Burns, Burns Night occurs on 25 January every year. Diners enjoy traditional Scottish fare such as haggis, as well as drinking Scotch whisky. Various toasts are given throughout the evening in which Scotch whisky is the drink of choice, especially when a male guest offers the traditional 'Toast to the Lassies'. One of the female guests then offers a witty speech and toast in return.

The quaich

Drinking whisky from the quaich is a long-held Scottish tradition. The name comes from the Gaelic word *cuach* meaning loving cup. Originating in the Highlands many centuries ago, the quaich is a shallow two-handled cup or bowl, usually engraved with Celtic designs and the owner's initials. It is used in official ceremonies, such as the 2014 Commonwealth Games, in 'wetting the baby's head' to celebrate newborns, at weddings and other similar occasions. The quaich is a popular wedding gift. In 1589, King James VI of Scotland gave a quaich to his new wife, Anne of Denmark.

Hot toddies

Hot toddies are the perfect answer to a cold night. A traditional drink, the toddy is designed to warm and comfort. Individual recipes can vary but generally making a toddy involves placing whisky and spices such as ginger in a glass, then adding hot water. Sir Walter Scott always enjoyed a hot toddy before bedtime.

2

GIN

GIN HISTORY

No one quite knows where gin originated, although it is known that medieval monks produced it as a medicinal drink. There are written references to 'genever' in *De Natura Rerum* (*The Nature of Things*) written by a thirteenth-century Dominican monk known as Thomas de Cantimpré. It seems to have originated in the Low Countries – an area covering what is now known as Holland, Belgium and Luxembourg. Records show that distilleries in Flanders were being taxed on genever production from the late fifteenth century onwards.

The first references to a gin-based recipe combining a variety of botanicals seems to have occurred in the Duchy of Guelders. Writing in *The Curious Bartender's Gin Palace*, Tristan Stephenson relates that

> In 1495, a wealthy merchant from a region known as the Duchy of Guelders (now part of the Netherlands, near Arnhem) decided it would be a good idea to have a book written for him. Being a household guide, the book documented some of the lavish recipes he and his family were enjoying at the time. Included was a brandy recipe made from '10 quarts of wine thinned with clear Hamburg beer'. After distillation, the liquid would be redistilled with 'two handfuls of dried sage, 1lb of cloves, 12 whole nutmegs, cardamom, cinnamon, galangal, ginger, grains of paradise' and – crucially – 'juniper berries'. The spices were placed in a cloth sack and suspended above the distillate, allowing the vapours to extract their flavour. Grinding diamonds over white truffle is as close a comparison as I can imagine to expressing the extravagance of such a recipe during that period. It's for this reason that it's highly unlikely that the drink was intended for anything other than sinful pleasures.

Extensive trade links between the Low Countries and England resulted in the importation and eventual production of genever in England and Scotland. By the late seventeenth century, genever had become extremely popular, especially among poorer people. Cheap to distil, it was a profitable way of using surplus grain. Many Scotch whisky producers exported fermented spirits southwards. So extensive was demand that between 1695 and 1735, the 'gin craze' in London led to many people drinking 10 litres or more of gin per year. It was cheaper to drink gin that any other drink, causing scenes of intoxication reflected in William Hogarth's well known engraving *Gin Lane*.

Gin has continued to be a popular mass market drink. In recent years, the number of producers has expanded considerably, along with a vast array of flavours and tastes. A gin renaissance began in the early years of the twenty-first century when the Gin Act was repealed, allowing the development of craft distilleries. In 2009, Sipsmith was the first small gin distillery to be established in London. By 2017, over 30,000 people had visited the Sipsmith distillery.

▲ ***'Margaret' the still, Dunnet Bay distillery.***
(© Dunnet Bay)

GIN PRODUCTION

Originally known as 'genever' or 'jenever', gin is produced by many whisky producers as it involves a similar initial production process. Smaller distillers often begin by producing gin as it does not require maturation, and so can be sold at a much earlier stage. Many whisky producers also provide the base liquid to specialist gin companies.

Gin is produced using a neutral spirit made from fermented grains, which is distilled in a traditional pot still. This is then redistilled together with a selection of botanicals (normally including juniper plus various herbs, spices, flowers and fruits), all designed to flavour the spirit.

The number of botanicals in gin varies considerably can involve ten or more options. The botanicals are usually steeped and boiled in the spirit for up to forty-eight hours, or are placed in baskets in modified

The juniper woodland at the Secret Garden distillery. (© Secret Garden) stills so as to combine with the spirit as vapour. Water is added to the condensed liquid to reduce the distilled spirit to bottling strength. Gins are usually ready for sale immediately on bottling.

One of the oldest gin brands still produced today is Diageo's Tanqueray.

Founded in 1830 by Charles Tanqueray, it is produced at the Cameronbridge distillery, beside the River Leven in Fife. The recipe for this Tanqueray London dry gin set the standard for all London dry gins ever since. One of the three copper pot stills used to make Tanqueray London dry has been in continuous use for over 250 years, having been first used in the reign of King George III. That particular still has been nicknamed 'Old Tom'.

In recent years, gin has undergone a renaissance, with distillers creating new styles that appeal to a much wider audience. Considerable innovation has taken place with new flavours being explored, as well as the introduction of attention grabbing colour-changing gins.

GIN LEGENDS

Dutch courage

This well known phrase dates back to the sixteenth and seventeenth centuries when English soldiers and sailors saw their Dutch compatriots drinking genever before battle. It gave them extra confidence – hence the phase 'Dutch courage'.

Old Tom

A popular name for a strong gin, this dates back to the eighteenth century. Among the possible origins of the name include the cat image used on Captain Dudley Bradstreet's wall-mounted gin vending system. Another story refers to a distiller named Thomas Chamberlin and his apprentice, Thomas Norris. When Norris (Young Tom) finished his apprenticeship, he decided to open a gin palace in Covent Garden. He named the gin on sale 'Old Tom' in honour of his former master, Thomas Chamberlain. What is definite is that Joseph Booard trademarked an Old Tom gin in 1849.

Bathtub gin

'Bathtub gin' is a popular name that originated in America during the Prohibition era in the 1920s. It referred to bottles of homemade gin filled from a bathtub. The term has since been used in films. In 2018, the film *Mary Poppins Returns* included a scene where Mary Poppins and the Banks children swim in a magical bathtub. Mary Poppins sings a song entitled 'Can You Imagine That?' in which the lyrics include the words:

Some people like to dive right in
Can you imagine that?
And flap about in bathtub gin
Can you imagine that?

Sailing around the world

In 1966, Sir Francis Chichester became the first person to single-handedly sail around the world, a journey of 15,500 miles. When organising his supplies, he included six bottles of gin and twenty-four bottles of assorted spirits. Chichester later credited his success at achieving that solo voyage to a daily glass of pink gin. The worst day of the trip was apparently when his supply of gin ran out.

Dennis Thatcher

One of the most well known gin drinkers was Dennis Thatcher, husband of Margaret, UK prime minister between 1979 and 1990. Typical Dennis Thatcher comments which entered the public domain included, 'I don't know what reception I'm at, but for God's sake, give me a gin and tonic.' On a morning flight to Scotland he apparently commented that 'it is never too early for a gin and tonic' while he told Downing Street staff to simply pass the cork of a bottle of Italian vermouth over his neat gin.

INSPIRED BY GIN

Ginspiration

Writer T.S. Eliot claimed that gin was one of his main sources of inspiration. In the *Letters of T.S. Eliot*, he explains how he came to write the monologue in *Sweeney Agonistes* saying, 'I wrote it in three quarters of an hour after church time, and before lunch one Sunday morning, with the assistance of half a bottle of Booth's gin.'

It is also reported that following a lecture at a small town near Boston, he was asked how he kept his youthful appearance. His reply became legendary: 'gin and drugs, Madam – gin and drugs!'

Noël Coward

Playwright Noël Coward referred to the importance of gin in his play *Words & Music*, when he had a group of debutantes singing:

The gin is lasting out,
No matter whose,
We're merely casting out
The Blues,
For gin, in cruel
Sober truth
Supplies the Fuel
For Flaming Youth,
A drink is known
To help a dream along
We can't refuse,
The gin is lasting out,
We're merely casting out
The Blues!

Medicinal gin

Drinking gin has benefited countless travellers and sailors over the past two centuries. Long voyages led to diseases such as scurvy due to the lack of vitamin C. When it was eventually discovered that lemon and lime juice made a difference, the Royal Navy decided to issue it to all its sailors. Unfortunately, it was also very bitter and acidic. Rear Admiral Sir Desmond Gimlette found a solution by mixing gin (designed to fortify) with Rose's lime cordial (to protect from scurvy) resulting in the Gimlet cocktail.

The Royal Navy unwittingly helped create another popular combination – the gin and tonic. Spread by mosquitos, malaria is endemic worldwide causing sufferers to experience serious illness which can be fatal. Treating it involved dissolving quinine in water and drinking it. The resultant mixture became known as tonic water – but it tasted horrible. To make it more palatable, the Royal Navy started adding gin, lemon juice and carbonated water. The result was Indian Tonic water, also popular, as noted earlier, with civilians travelling from England to India. According to Winston Churchill, 'the gin and tonic saved more Englishmen's lives, and minds, than all the doctors in the Empire'.

Mobile gin marketing

Edinburgh-based gin distiller Pickering's has taken gin to new levels with its unusual marketing methods. Its 'botanical engineers' have devised

▲ ***Pickering's gin Tip Top Tippling Trunk.*** (© Pickering's)

innovative gins and promotional materials such as the 'Tip Top Tippling Trunk', forming the essential kit for a gin salesman/botanical engineer. They adapted an old trunk acquired in a junk shop to hold all the paraphernalia of gin tasting, including three bottles of Pickering's gin, lights, music and stickers from their travels. A 650cc four-wheel drive Daihatsu Hi-Jet Japanese airport fire engine acquired on eBay has been re-engineered as a 'Thirst Extinguisher', dispensing gin and cocktails from the hoses.

Pickering's 'Monkeybike' is the smallest mobile gin bar worldwide, while its 'Marvellously Mixed Musical Martini Maker, Mark II' is made from a wind-up gramophone, an American lamp from the 1940s, chemistry equipment from the 1960s and a coffee cafetière found in a charity shop. Even the labels on the unique square-tapered bottles with curved edges required special treatment. According to the company it was 'a bugger to wrap a label around'. Yet, rather than change the bottle shape, Pickering's invented its own machine to affix the labels perfectly every time: 'She was only meant to label batch one. She managed 100,000 bottles of Pickering's gin before we retired her in 2016.'

▲ ***The Fire Engine Bar at Pickering's.*** (© Pickering's)

▲ ***The Monkeybike.*** (© Pickering's)

The Marvellously Mixed Musical Martini Maker. (© Pickerings)

INVESTING AND TASTING

BOTTLE DESIGN

Both whisky and gin are traditionally sold in glass bottles, with a wide range of styles and designs being utilised, some of which are collectible. Among the more distinctive shapes are triangular bottles from Glenfiddich, fluted versions from the Isle of Harris and compact bottles imprinted with fossils and stones from Raasay. There have also been unusual examples such as bottles that light up, a skull-shaped decanter, memento mori and

▲ ***Glenturret whisky bottles.*** (© Glenturret)

a double-barrel design. Some of the rarest whiskies have appeared in very distinctive packaging – for example, bottles of sixty-year-old 1926 The Macallan have artwork hand-painted by the Irish artist Michael Dillon.

Gin bottles have been equally innovative, including two-toned colours, square bottles, embossed wine bottle styles at Lind & Lime and, at Linlithgow, bottles that tell the story of the town. LinGin set out to pay homage to St Magdalene's, the last whisky distillery in the town, and featured the distillery's distinctive cupola top. The bottle shape itself reflects the historic spire of St Michael's church, while turning the bottle over reveals the crown of thorns spire on the bottom of the bottle.

One of the more unusual heritage bottle styles can be seen at Brodie Castle, now in the care of the National Trust for Scotland. During the nineteenth century there was a trend for wealthy households to possess specially made decanters for use with individual types of alcohol. At Brodie Castle, the tradition was to use 'gin pigs'. The clear decanter was picked up by the pig's tail, and the drink poured out through the pig's nose, which is marked by a cork stopper. It was a style that was resurrected for a short while in the 2020s by glass company Angels' Share Glass as a distinctive type of gift bottle.

▲ ***Johnny Walker Blue Label Ultra.*** (© Diageo)

An innovation in whisky bottles occurred in 2024 when Diageo (a British multinational alcoholic beverage company) introduced a new patented design in the form of a Johnnie Walker Blue Label ultra-lightweight bottle weighing just 180g (without a stopper) for a 70cl bottle. This is considerably different to the more conventional whisky bottles weighing in the region of 400g–1,000g. Even the traditional Johnnie Walker Blue Label bottle weights 850g.

This new lightweight bottle was the result of five years of testing, exploring all aspects of bottle manufacture and transportation. The Johnnie Walker Blue Label 'Ultra' bottle has an elegant teardrop shape, moulded to mimic the iconic square Johnnie Walker bottles by providing a protective cage for the round base. These bottles are experimental and available in a limited edition of 888 bottles sold around the world in select markets during 2025.

Diageo indicated that this experimental bottle was a small-scale production, but it indicates what could be achieved in terms of making bottles much more sustainable in the long term. Lighter glass bottles means less glass needs to be produced, thus reducing energy and emissions on transportation.

A popular option taken up by some distillers, especially gin producers such as Dunnett Bay, has been the introduction of refill packs. Drinkers can purchase refill pouches, which simply have to be poured into the empty bottle. In addition, visitors to the Dunnet Bay distillery can bring their empty bottles and refill them on site at the distillery shop.

In general terms, distillers are becoming increasingly focused on sustainability, encouraging bottles to be reused or recycled.

INVESTING IN WHISKY

Whisky has become increasingly popular as an investment. Often people will buy a bottle to drink and a matching bottle to invest. Prices can be very high, and this has resulted in thefts occurring. In 2022, twenty bottles of rare whisky valued at over £150,000 were stolen from the Glenfarclass distillery, Ballindalloch. To date, none of the bottles have appeared worldwide, and it is believed that they have just been hidden away. No one has been apprehended for the crime.

The Macallan brand has been reaching extremely high figures at auction. In 2014, The Macallan M Imperiale 6-litre Lalique (a single malt scotch whisky in a Lalique crystal decanter) was auctioned in Hong Kong for a staggering $628,205. This was exceeded at Sotheby's in London on 24 October 2019 when a bottle of The Macallan 1926 sold for £1,452,000 ($1,811,250). Four years later, in 2023, Guinness World Records noted that

▲ ***One of the rarest collections of Scotch whisky is located at The Scotch Whisky Experience in Edinburgh.*** (The Scotch Whisky Experience)

this record price was smashed again at Sotheby's when a bottle of The Macallan Valerio Adami 60 Year Old 1926 was sold to an anonymous bidder for £2,187,500 ($2,734,524). The 1926 is one of the most sought after Scotch whiskies. Only forty bottles were ever produced, of which twelve were designed by the Italian painter Valerio Adami.

By far the largest collection of rare whisky can be seen at The Scotch Whisky Experience in Edinburgh, and the sheer rarity of the bottles makes it impossible to put a price on the collection. Among the incredibly rare bottles on display are the centenary Strathmill single malt of which only 100 bottles were produced. None were sold as all the bottles were given away to heads of state such as Queen Elizabeth II, the president of the USA and some industry specialists like Claive Videz, who was the original owner of the collection.

Apart from investing in individual bottles of whisky, many collectors are also opting for private casks. This is a practice that is being increasingly offered by distilleries. In general, it involves a distillery releasing a limited number of private casks on a first come, first served basis. Ardgowan distillery is one such company offering this service. The cask is filled with new-make spirit (clear, unaged, and undiluted liquid from the still) and held for ten years in its bonded warehouse. Additional services may be provided to investors in the form of access to exclusive distillery events, advice on bottling, samples on request, visits, and an option for the distillery to buy back casks at the end of the period.

Distilleries often set apart special casks for long-term investment. In 1998, actor Ewan McGregor visited Lochranza distillery on the Isle of Arran to toast the first cask of Arran single malt. This was the first legal cask to be laid down on Arran for over 150 years. Lochranza also presented him with his own ex-sherry hogshead which was left to mature in the Lochranza warehouse until 2024 when it was bottled. The first twenty-four bottles of this rare twenty-six-year-old whisky were personally signed by Ewan McGregor and then auctioned for charity in aid of Children's Hospices Across Scotland (CHAS).

Anyone considering investing in whisky would be advised to seek professional help and advice. Casks, for example, have to be stored in a government bonded warehouse, together with a clearly identifiable official paper trail for each and every cask. The value of any particular whisky bottle or cask depends mainly on scarcity of supply together with rising demand for a particular brand or bottle. Prices can go down as well as up. Whisky is also a long-term investment, with the best whisky having been aged in barrels for up to twenty years or more. The majority of whiskies will not appreciate greatly in value, and should only be regarded as a personal investment for future drinking.

WHAT MAKES A RARE SCOTCH WHISKY?

Age is a key factor. The older the whisky, the more complex the flavours and depths, but not all old whiskies are deemed rare, even though they are more costly to produce. The whisky is old because it has had to be matured for longer, and kept unsold under the correct conditions in warehouses, taking up space and hence costing the distiller money.

When looking for a rare Scotch whisky, searching out limited editions can be a good option. These are generally highly prized, especially if they represent a good year and possess a unique flavour. Frequently, these limited editions are created from single casks – which means the amount of whisky that can be bottled from that cask is immediately limited. One standard barrel may well produce only 200 7cl bottles.

▲ ***Brora's 44 year old Untold Depths.*** (Brora)

By far the most sought after whiskies are bottles from lost or closed distilleries. These bottles represent never to be repeated brands and tastes, as the distillery will (probably) not be making whisky again. But there is always a risk if choosing such a whisky for investment. Many larger distillers have been known to close a distillery by 'mothballing' it – stopping production but leaving the distillery in place, giving them the option of reopening at some time in the future if demand warrants it. Port Ellen was one such lost distillery. It was closed in 1983, but everything was left in place, turning it into a ghost distillery. A rare cask of Port Ellen whisky that had been distilled in 1979 was auctioned at Sotheby's in 2022 for £875,000. In 2024, Port Ellen reopened as a full-scale distillery including a visitor centre.

VISITING DISTILLERIES

Visiting a distillery can be a fantastic way to talk to experts, discover its history, heritage and production methods and sample the produce. It is a great way to explore different

Brora distillery tour experience. (Brora)

tastes and learn how spirits differ from region to region, even within a few miles, depending on the type of water and soil.

Not all distilleries are open to the public, usually as a result of limited space, so it is important to check beforehand as to what facilities are provided. Tours and special experiences such as a visit to a dunnage warehouse require pre-booking, as numbers on each tour are limited. During the high summer season, or during festivals, such tours and experiences are often fully booked many weeks ahead so pre-planning is essential.

One of the big advantages of exploring distilleries is the opportunity to taste and try new varieties. The usual recommendation is to begin by admiring the colour. This reflects the maturation process and the type of casks used. The darker the whisky, the older it usually is. Swirl the liquid around the glass and breathe in the aromas. Take a sip and hold in the mouth for about ten seconds in order to experience the full flavour of the drink. Try neat first, and then add water to see how it changes. Special driver's packs are usually available at visitor centres enabling drivers to safely enjoy the tour and take home samples for trialling.

Tasting session at Glen Scotia distillery. (Glen Scotia)

Dunnet Bay distillery shop. (Dunnet Bay)

Distillery shops provide a wide range of related products, often including special limited editions. Local merchandise is also frequently available.

TRAVELLING AROUND SCOTLAND

Be prepared to travel some distance to visit distilleries. Although many can be accessed by public transport in towns and cities like Edinburgh, Glasgow and Aberdeen, bear in mind that many others are located in remote areas. There may be little or no public transport available. When visiting islands, such as Jura and the Orkneys, access is by ferry so it is worth checking in advance the times and availability of ferry crossings.

Plan your journeys in advance to ensure that distilleries are open. Guided tours and other experiences usually have to be booked well before time, and events such as whisky festivals are likely to be booked out many months in advance. If you plan to combine several distilleries during your trip, you will need to include travelling time. In winter, roads may be inaccessible due to bad weather. Distances can be deceptive, as roads can be narrow and involve sea crossings and mountain ranges, as well as urban areas.

▼ ***Remote locations like that of the Crafty distillery are common in Scotland.*** (Crafty)

▲ ***Sculptures make a distinctive feature outside Rosebank distillery.*** (© Rosebank)

ANNUAL FESTIVALS

Every year there are many whisky and gin festivals held throughout the country. Among the most well known annual festivals are the following.

Braemar Whisky Festival
www.braemarwhiskyfestival.com

Held in October, the festival seeks to celebrate the cultural heritage of Braemar while giving back to the local community. The festival includes tastings, masterclasses and expert-led discussions, and showcases the range of whiskies produced in the area. Other events include an opportunity to retrace the steps of illicit distillers, complete with ponies and drams.

Campbeltown Malts Festival
www.springbank.scot/malts-festival-info

This is held annually each May, offering a series of events such as tastings and tours linked to the different distilleries. Booking in advance is recommended.

Dornoch Whisky Festival
www.dornochwhiskyfestival.com

Taking place in October, this weekend festival focuses on how Dornoch evolved into a whisky hub. The festival takes place at the Dornoch Castle Hotel. There are masterclasses, tasting sessions and the opportunity to sample a wide range of whiskies from throughout Scotland.

Fife Whisky Festival
www.fifewhiskyfestival.com

Taking place in March, this festival is based in Cupar, with additional events taking place in various locations and distilleries in the region. It features immersive tastings, an on-site retailer, an exhibition involving over forty distilleries and bottlers, all offering samples, visits to bonded warehouses and an opening dinner. Separate tickets have to be obtained for each event.

Fèis Ile – Islay Whisky Festival
www.feisile.co.uk

An extremely popular festival, Fèis Ile has been running since 1985 and attracts visitors from around the world. The aim is to encourage an appreciation of the heritage of Islay and its whisky distilleries. Distillery tours are available including the iconic Laphroaig and Lagavulin distilleries. There is also lots of traditional music along with community events. The festival normally takes place around the end of May or beginning of June. Tickets have to be purchased for individual events rather than the overall festival.

International Scottish Gin Day
www.internationalscottishginday.com

Established by The Gin Co-operative, International Scottish gin Day is a major celebration of everything related to Scottish gin. It takes place in early October, and attracts consumers, retailers, bar-owners and Scottish gin producers. Events take place nationwide, providing an opportunity to try exclusive cocktails and food and gin pairings, as well as meeting distillers and enjoying plenty of sampling.

Spirit of Speyside
www.spiritofspeyside.com

Taking place in May, this large-scale, week-long festival celebrates Speyside whisky production. The first festival was held in 1999, and it has evolved into one of the biggest such festivals in Scotland. It provides a fantastic opportunity to discover distilleries, such as Tamnavulin, which are normally closed to the public, as well as trying new whiskies. There are many exclusive tastings, blending workshops and masterclasses which can be booked in advance. Other activities include

Spirit of Speyside festival. (Spirit of Speyside)

food, talks, ceilidhs, art exhibitions, live music and opportunities to enjoy the outdoors by trying off-roading, trail running and canoeing.

Stirling SpiritFest
www.stirlingdistllery.com/pages/spiritfest

Held at the end of October/beginning of November, the SpiritFest combines a gin and a whisky festival. It has become one of the most popular autumn events, attracting lots of visitors keen to sample different spirits, participate in masterclasses and discover more about the world of gin and whisky.

WHISKY AND GIN HOTELS

There are now hotels linked specifically to whisky and gin, creating a very unique overnight experience.

Borodale House
www.raasaydistillery.com

Borodale House, at the Isle of Raasay distillery in the Hebrides, is the only place in Scotland where you can stay overnight at a working distillery. A former Victorian villa located on the site has been transformed into a whisky hotel with six en-suite double bedrooms. Borodale House was originally designed in the 1800s by Alexander Ross and has been recently restored, combining heritage with modern life. Visitors are able to wake up to stunning views of the Cuillin Mountains as well as the distillery staff creating new batches of whisky and gin.

Craigellachie Hotel
www.craigellachiehotel.com

A hotel possessing an undeniable whisky history! Set amid beautiful countryside, Craigellachie Hotel is home to the oldest pub in Speyside, the Spey Inn. This is an old drovers' inn dating back to 1703 and now acts as both a pub and a restaurant for the hotel. The Spey Inn produces its own Copper Dog whisky and uses only locally sourced ingredients in the restaurant.

Also on site is the legendary Quaich Bar, possessing over 1,000 single malt whiskies as well as offering superb iconic cocktails. The Quaich Bar was founded over 120 years ago. The name comes from the traditional Scottish two-handled quaich drinking vessel, which denotes friendship and hospitality. Full of green velvet sofas and red leather chairs, this is a bar where visitors are spoilt for choice when choosing a dram of whisky. Fortunately, bespoke whisky tastings and whisky flights (selections of multiple whiskies served in small amounts) are carefully curated by the bar manager.

Dornoch Castle Hotel
www.dornochcastlehotel.com

Located in the town of Dornoch, the hotel is part of a historic castle and is well known for its involvement in the whisky industry. Every October, it hosts a Scotch whisky festival attracting considerable attention from keen whisky drinkers. Accommodation is available both within the castle and in nearby self-catering holiday cottages. The Dornoch Castle Whisky Bar is sited in the centre of the castle, and has gained international acclaim for the range of rare and unique whiskies on offer. Visitors can participate in specially curated whisky tasting flights. There is even a special range of whisky and gin produced in the grounds of the hotel.

Kinloch Lodge
www.kinloch-lodge.co.uk

Kinloch Lodge collaborates with the nearby Torabhaig distillery to offer a 'Sense of Place' package. This includes accommodation, a Torabhaig tour and tasting, a whisky-themed picnic lunch, a foraging walk and a cocktail-making class.

Loch Leven Hotel
www.pixelspiritsltd.co.uk

Sited at the foot of Glencoe, Loch Leven Hotel is a historic inn which dates back to the seventeenth century. A family-run

Loch Leven Hotel. (© Loch Leven/Pixel Spirits)

hotel, it operates a craft distillery in the grounds, producing a range of gins, rums and vodkas such as the Devil's Staircase Highland spiced gin. Distillery tours and tasting sessions are available, and visitors can try the spirits in the hotel bar. In addition to the Pixel spirits, the Old Ferry Bar also stocks a wide range of Scottish whiskies.

Loch Ness Drumnadrochit Hotel
www.lochnessdrumnadrochit.cobbshotels.com

Part of the Loch Ness complex, the Drumnadrochit Hotel is where the modern stories of Nessie first began. In 1933, Mrs Aldie MacKay reported seeing a 'water beast' in the loch, sparking a media frenzy that has continued ever since, with visitors hoping to spot the elusive Loch Ness Monster. Nowadays, the Drumnadrochit hotel complex contains a variety of attractions including a distillery where visitors can enjoy gin flights, talks, tours and other related experiences.

Peebles Hydro Hotel
www.peebleshydro.co.uk

Since 1881, Peebles Hydro has been providing hotel accommodation to

Peebles Hydro Hotel. (© Peebles Hydro)

visitors keen on taking advantage of its clear spring waters. It is now part of the Crieff Family of hotels and the extensive grounds provide a variety of bookable experiences such as axe-throwing and archery. There are also opportunities for gin distillery tours and bespoke workshops, since the 1881 gin distillery, complete with a gin school, is located in the grounds.

The Torridon
www.thetorridon.com

Deep in the Highlands, the Torridon resort includes a hotel with a variety of experiences such as a whisky nosing and tasting experience from a selection of over 365 malts as well as a gin experience. The Torridon has its own distillery creating Arcturus gin.

Torrisdale Castle Estate
www.torrisdalecastle.com

A small family-owned estate complete with its own castle and distillery (the Beinn an Tuirc Distillers), Torrisdale offers opportunities for guests to take part in a gin school and a tour of the distillery, as well as enjoying the beauty of Kintyre and Torrisdale Bay. Accommodation is provided in the form of self-catering 'eco-bothies', cottages and a unique castle apartment.

▾ ***Stepherds' and bakers' bothies at Torrisdale.*** (© Torrisdale)

WHISKY AND GIN DISTILLERIES OPEN TO THE PUBLIC, BY WHISKY REGION

When setting out to visit a distillery, check that it is actually open to the public. Not all distilleries offer visitor facilities. Some may have on-site shops but no other visitor access; some may offer guided tours or other experiences on a regular or occasional basis.

CAMPBELTOWN

CADENHEAD'S

9 Bolgam Street
Campbeltown,
PA28 6HU
www.cadenhead.scot

Founded in 1842, Cadenhead's is a wine and spirits merchant with branches in Edinburgh and London. It is now owned by the Mitchell's group which operates the Springbank and Glengyle distilleries. Apart from buying a wide range of wines and spirits on site, visitors can take part in a range of special experiences.

Located behind the Cadenhead's shop, the Tasting Room offers the chance to sample numerous Cadenhead bottlings, as well as a range of wines, beers, cocktails and soft drinks. It is open daily.

Visitors can book a Cadenhead's 'Warehouse Tasting' offering the opportunity to experience drams from all over the world.

'Cadenhead's Creation' offers an unusual blending session inside the new Cadenhead's lab. Visitors have to use their senses to create the perfect personal blend, as none of the different cask types are labelled. The result is a 70cl hand-blended bottle to take home.

BEINN AN TUIRC
Lephincorrach Farm,
Torrisdale,
Carradale,
Campbeltown
PA28 6QT
www.kintyregin.com

An aerial view of Torrisdale Castle, Beinn an Tuiric distillery and Torrisdale Castle Estate. (© Torrisdale)

Established in 2016 on the Torrisdale Castle Estate, Beinn an Tuirc aims to be as sustainable as possible with all water sourced from the highest point on the peninsula, the Beinn an Tuirc Hill (the Hill of the Wild Boar), which is above the distillery building. The distillery's main product is Kintyre gin which includes two local unique botanicals: Icelandic moss and sheep sorrel. Book a Kintyre gin experience offering a tour of the distillery, its history and gin sampling.

Located on Kintyre's scenic east coast, Beinn an Tuirc is about twelve miles from Cambeltown. Self-catering accommodation is provided, with a licensed distillery café and access to Torrisdale Bay, which is perfect for water sports, wild swimming and wildlife watching. Go to www.torrisdalecastle.com for more details.

GLENGYLE
Mitchell's Glengyle Ltd
9 Bolgam Street
Campbeltown
PA28 6HZ
www.kilkerran.scot

Glengyle has had a chequered history. Originally linked to a local

▲ ***Emma Macallister at the distillery.*** (© Beinn An Tuiric)

family-based distilling and farming business, one of its members – William Mitchell – decided to set up his own separate distillery in the late 1800s. Ownership of Glengyle changed hands twice in the twentieth century, before the distillery closed down. The buildings remained well preserved, resulting in several attempts to revive the distillery. In 2000, Hedley G. Wright, chairman of Springbank and the great-great grand nephew of William Mitchell, the original founder, purchased the site and opened Mitchell's Glengyle. Its Kilkerran single malt whisky is named in honour of St Kerran who lived in the area.

Three guided experiences are available linking Kilkerran with the Springbank distillery. Advance booking is recommended. The 'Cadenhead's Warehouse Tasting' offers an opportunity sample a selection of Cadenhead's whiskies from various distilleries in a traditional warehouse. The 'Kilkerran' tour explores the distillery and the whisky-making process, plus sampling a whisky. The 'Springbank' tour is a distillery tour and sampling session.

▼ ***Glen Scotia distillery.*** (© Glen Scotia)

GLEN SCOTIA
12 High Street
Campbeltown
PA28 6DS
www.glenscotia.com

Part of the Loch Lomond Group, Glen Scotia is a small distillery dating back to the 1830s, with a historic mash tun, still room and dunnage warehouse. It produces two types of whisky, peated and non-peated, together with a range of malts, festival edition whiskies and limited edition seasonal single malts. Tastes vary from sweet and fruity to rich and smoky.

Tours of the distillery can be booked, exploring what goes on behind the scenes and combined with a complimentary dram of double cask single malt whisky. The 'Dunnage Warehouse' experience offers a longer, more immersive tour combined with a whisky tasting. The 'Distillery Manager' tour is described as the ultimate experience covering the working distillery grounds and led by the manager himself. This is concluded with a tasting of five whiskies drawn straight from hand-selected casks in the warehouse.

▲ ***Iain McAllister, master distiller, checking the Glen Scotia whisky.*** (© Glen Scotia)

MACHRIHANISH
Dhurrie Farm
Campbeltown
PA28 6NT
www.machrihanishdistillery.com

This is the first farm distillery to be opened in the area for over 180 years. It offers true field-to-bottle quality incorporating a net zero production process to create a contemporary Campbeltown single malt whisky. The intention is to use biological farming practices and create greater biodiversity on the farmland.

Machrihanish is owned by R&B Distillers, which also operates the Isle

Springbank distillery. (© Springbank)

of Raasay distillery. There is a visitor centre and whisky club.

SPRINGBANK
Well Close
Campbeltown
PA28 6ET
www.springbank.scot

Springbank is the oldest independent family-owned distillery in Scotland. It was founded in 1828 on the site of an illicit still operated by Archibald Mitchell, a member of a long established local family. The distillery managed to survive the changing tastes and recession of the twentieth century and by the late 1990s experienced increased demand for its products. New whisky ranges such as Hazelburn and Longrow were introduced while its core lightly peated and two-and-a-half times distilled Springbank single malt has been produced since 1828. The distillery still uses traditional skills passed through the generations.

A range of distillery tours and tastings are available including the 'Kilkerran' tour, the 'Springbank' tour and the 'Barley to Bottle' tour, plus other tours and experiences linked to

▲ ***Springbank tasting session.*** (© Springbank from barreltobottle)

the Cadenhead whisky shop. Visitors are welcome at the Washback Bar to try tasting flights and whiskies, new releases and rare archive whiskies as well as enjoy lunchtime snacks.

The Springbank Whisky School provides an opportunity to experience traditional distilling methods.

WATT WHISKY
51 Kirk Street
Campbeltown
PA28 6BW
www.wattwhisky.com

Watt Whisky is an independent bottling company dealing with single malt, blended malt, single grain, blended rums and Indian whisky. It uses casks from a range of distillers from across Scotland as well as a range of spirits from elsewhere such as an Armagnac from Chateau Laubade.

Watt Whisky organises various events such as the 'Liquid History' walking tour and 'Rainbow Tasting' during the annual Campbeltown Malts Festival.

HIGHLAND

8 DOORS
John O'Groats,
Caithness,
KW1 4YR
www.8doorsdistillery.com

Scotland's most northerly mainland distillery is situated at the iconic John O'Groats and possesses stunning scenic views. John O'Groats is a small coastal village at the most northerly point of the UK. The 8 Doors distillery began distilling whisky in 2022, the first to be made in John O'Groats for over 180 years. Water used in the whisky comes from an on-site borehole.

8 doors distillery. (© 8 doors)

The sea mist, ocean spray and cool temperatures experienced at John O'Groats ensure that the maturation process creates a complex range of flavours and characteristics. Product ranges include the hand-crafted Five Ways liqueur and the Seven Sons range of blended Scotch whisky.

The distillery name was inspired by the legend of Jan de Groot and the house he built on a mound near the John O'Groats House Hotel. The house was octagonal and had eight doors, one for each of his sons and himself, leading to an eight-sided table so that no one could occupy the head of the table, thus avoiding family arguments.

Coffee, cakes, cocktails and soft drinks can be purchased in the lounge area, which also includes a whisky bar. There is an on-site shop.

Varying options for distillery tours are available ranging from a full tasting tour, to enjoying a flight of whisky samples in the dedicated tasting room overlooking the stills. Some tours are bookable online, others involve walk-in bookings only. Drivers receive a miniature bottle from the Seven Sons range.

ABHAINN DEARG
Carnish
Uig
Isle of Lewis
Outer Hebrides
HS2 9EX
www.abhainndeargdistillery.co.uk

Abhainn Dearg is the most westerly of all the Scottish distilleries. When it launched its first single malt in 2011, it was the first to be produced on the Isle of Lewis since 1844. The malted barley is grown on Uig, ensuring field-to-bottle artisanal production. After distillation, the spirit is placed in bourbon oak and European sherry casks to mature. The company uses only traditional methods, filtering the spirit, filling and labelling bottles by hand (even the miniatures). The whisky has no added colour and is not chill-filtered.

There is a whisky shop on site. Pre-booked distillery tours are available and include a guided tour plus sample tastings.

ARBIKIE HIGHLAND ESTATE
Lunan Bay
Montrose
Angus
DD10 9TR
www.arbikie.com

A family-owned business, located on the east coast of Angus, Arbikie operates on field-to-bottle principles. Almost everything used in the production of its products is grown and produced on the farm, including juniper and honey. The distillery itself is sited in an ancient barn. Arbikie aims to be sustainable and eco-friendly, using solar power and with all primary waste products from the distilling being recycled as cattle feed. It is the world's first hydrogen-powered distillery, possessing a wind turbine, electrolyser, hydrogen storage and hydrogen boiler system. The company created the world's first 'climate positive' gin and vodka known as Nàdar, and the first Scottish rye whisky in 200 years.

There is a visitor centre on site, a café, plus accommodation that can be pre-booked. Visitors can try a gin and vodka experience, a cocktail experience and a whisky experience. The distillery hosts frequent events such as live music and comedy nights.

Other distilleries in Angus: Angus Alchemy, Glencadam, Toll House Spirits/ Redcastle

ARDGOWAN
Bankfoot Farm
Inverkip
Renfrewshire
PA16 0DT
www.ardgowandistillery.com

Ardgowan is located at the junction of the Highland and Lowland regions, close to the sea and the warming effects of the Gulf Stream. A newly constructed distillery, it is part of the historic Ardgowan Estate, near the village of Inverkip. Production is scheduled to start in 2025, and will ultimately produce over 1,000,000 litres of malt whisky annually. The distillery has been built to be as sustainable as possible, utilising a heat recovery system as well as CO_2 capture from fermentation in order to make the distillery carbon neutral. It is the home of Ardgowan's unique 'Infinity Cask', which is specially designed for super-long maturation, recapturing the golden era of sherry cask matured whisky. Ardgowan plans to create a range of high quality whiskies and gins alongside the Clydebuilt range of single malts and Clydebuilt Scottish dry gin, first produced in 2024.

The new distillery will include a purpose-built visitor centre. Open days are held and details are available from the website.

▾ ***Arndamurchan distillery viewed from above.*** (© Ardnamuchan)

ARDNAMURCHAN
Glenbeg
Ardnamurchan
Argyll
PH36 4JG
www.adelphidistillery.com

One of the most remote distilleries in Scotland, Ardnamurchan is situated on the Ardnamurchan peninsula of Lochaber. The distillery is owned by Adelphi, an independent bottling company. Production started in 2014, and its first official whisky was released in 2017. It is a sustainable distillery powered by hydro-electricity and biomass, and uses barley from one of the owner's estates. Water is drawn from a spring above the distillery and residues from production are used as fertiliser or feed for herds. Both peated and unpeated whiskies are produced on site. Flavours are intense and the whisky is bottled at cask strength.

Ardnamurchan has a visitor centre and shop, open six days a week. There is a range of distillery tours including the 'Behind the Scenes' tour. Booking is recommended.

Other distilleries in Argyll:
Nc'Nean, Oban

▼ ***Ardnamurchan warehouse with barrels of whisky.*** (© Ardnamurchan)

ANGUS ALCHEMY
Woodhill
Carnoustie
Angus
DD7 7SD
www.angusalchemy.com

This is not a traditional distillery, but describes itself as being 'distillers of divergence'. Martin, Phil and Campbell are entrepreneurs and the self-described 'Masters of Mayhem' behind Angus Alchemy. They created their own distillery involving cutting-edge design and operations in order to produce world-class gin, rum and moonshine. Among the selections on offer are Banoffee Pie moonshine, Prickly gin, Clootie Biscoff Chippie moonshine and Cranachan moonshine.

Visitors can book distillery tours complete with tasting sessions. There is a tasting package comprising selections from all the whisky regions as well as a tasting session focusing on the range of alcohol produced at Angus, from gin to mezcal. There are opportunities to explore the angels' share, the *uisge beatha* (water of life) and a barrel bonanza. Bespoke tours and experiences can also be provided.

Other distilleries in Angus: Arbikie, Glencadam, Toll House Spirits/ Redcastle

BADACHRO
Badachro
Gairloch
Ross and Cromarty
IV21 2AA
www.badachro.co.uk

Badachro is a small, independent family-owned distillery located in the small village of Badachro, offering scenic views across to Skye. The village is on the shore of Gair Loch. Badachro produces a selection of whiskies, gins and vodkas. These include Coastal gin, Madeira cask finish whisky, Ruby Oak whisky and Tuscan Oak whisky.

Pre-booked, introductory tour and tasting experiences are available. Self-catering accommodation in a timber-built chalet is also available at the distillery itself.

Other distilleries in Ross and Cromarty: Balblair, Dalmore, Fairytale, Glenmorangie, Singleton of Glen Ord

BALBLAIR
Edderton
Tain
Ross and Cromarty
IV19 1LB
www.balblair.com

Established in 1790 by John Ross, a local businessman on the estate of the Rosses of Balnagown, Balblair grew rapidly following the arrival of the railways. Production slumped in the 1930s leading to its closure. It was subsequently occupied by the Norwegian Army for the duration of the Second World War. Production resumed in 1948, and it was subsequently sold to new owners. By 2007, Balblair had been purchased by Inver House Distillers, and has since grown steadily, releasing unique age statement expressions of its whisky.

The distillery is located on a remote hillside overlooking Dornoch Firth, which was used over 3,000 years ago as an ancient Pictish gathering place. A Pictish standing stone from that period still sits beside the distillery, and the iconic 'Z Rod' marking is symbolised on each bottle of Balblair whisky. The company produces single malts from slow distillation, possessing a very distinct light flavour with fruity, leathery and nutty characteristics reflecting the use of Black Isle barley and the open water from the Edderton Hills.

Guided tours of the distillery incorporating a tasting session can be booked. There is a visitor centre on site.

Other distilleries in Ross and Cromarty: Badachro, Dalmore, Fairytale, Glenmorangie, Singleton of Glen Ord

BEN NEVIS
Lochy Bridge
Fort William
Inverness-shire
PH33 6TJ
www.bennevisdistillery.com

Located at the base of Ben Nevis, the highest mountain in the UK, the distillery was founded in 1825. It was one of the first to experiment with continuous distillation, and also one of the first to produce both grain and malt whisky. It produces strong, peated whisky flavoured with the honey and heather of the moors. The company undertakes bottling for various other companies. Not surprisingly, the pot stills are extremely large and capable of distilling over 25,000 litres. Yet more whisky is distilled in smaller spirit stills, providing a fast distillation process. The Ben Nevis distillery is owned by the Japanese Whisky company Nikka.

The 'Legend of the Dew of Ben Nevis' visitor centre is situated in an old distillery warehouse on site. Open all year, it contains an audio-visual presentation involving Hector McDram, a mythical giant who tells the story of the legend of the dew of Ben Nevis. Visitors are then given a guided tour of the production areas and a complimentary tasting of the whisky.

Also on site is a coffee shop, a restaurant and a shop containing a range of local gifts, treats and, of course, whisky.

Other distilleries in Invernes-shire: Dalwhinnie, Great Glen, Kinrara, Pixel Spirits, Tomatin, Uile-Bheist

BLAIR ATHOL
Perth Road,
Pitlochry,
Perthshire
PH16 5LY
www.malts.com/en-gb/distilleries/blair-athol

Pitlochry is a picturesque location in the foothills of the Grampian Mountains surrounded by moorland. The Allt Dour Burn flows from the slopes of Ben Vrakie through the grounds of the distillery. The use of this water contributes its flavour to the smooth, mellow whisky produced here. The distillery was founded in 1798, and is now part of the Diageo group. It produces a single malt whisky available as a 12-year-old bottling, and it is also used in Bell's whisky.

Guided tours of the distillery can be booked, as well as a 'Cask and Cocktail' experience. There is a distillery shop on site.

Other distilleries in Perthshire: Deanston, Dewars, Eradour, Gatehouse Gin, Glenturret, Pert, Persie, Toulvaddie, Tulibardine

Brora distillery. (© Brora)

BRORA
Brora
Tain
Sutherland
KW9 6LR
www.malts.com/en-gb/distilleries/brora

Founded in 1819 by the Marquess of Stafford, Brora produced peated single malt whisky until 1983, when the then owners, The Distillers Company, decided to mothball the site. For many years it was regarded as a ghost distillery, until in 2001 the decision was made to restore production, which resumed in 2021. Prior to this, the site was comprehensively restored. The 202-year-old stillhouse was taken down and rebuilt exactly as it was when first opened in 1819, and the copper stills were refurbished by Diageo's coppersmiths. It is now a carbon-neutral distillery powered by on-site renewable energy. Brora has the capacity to produce a maximum of 800,000 litres of spirit annually. Brora marked the third anniversary of its restoration with the launch of a forty-four-year-old distillery exclusive single malt Scotch whisky called Untold Depths.

Discover how the distillery came back to life after thirty-eight years with a distillery tour. These are available by appointment only. Visitors have the opportunity to experience tastings of, and purchase, rare Brora releases. The tours have to be pre-booked. On-site retail sales are only available to people taking part in the tours.

Other distilleries in Sutherland: Clynelish, Dornoch

CITY OF ABERDEEN
Arch 10
Palmerston Road
Aberdeen
AB11 5RE
www.cityofaberdeendistillery.co.uk

City of Aberdeen is an independent distillery, owned and operated by two friends – Dan and Alan. It was the first distillery to be opened in Aberdeen for nearly eighty years. It is also home to the Aberdeen gin school. The distillery, school and shop were all founded in 2019.

All the gins are made with premium organic alcohol, resulting in gins that are smooth and sweet. Locally grown fruit and botanicals are also used. City of Aberdeen has become known for its unusual tastes, especially on a seasonal basis. Regular gins include Thyme for Rosemary (made to accompany Italian food), Signature Aberdeen (telling the story of Aberdeen around the bottle using stencil drawings) and 1860 (based on a recipe discovered at the height of the Victorian era). Among the more unusual options that have been created are Curry gin (which does taste like curry), Chocolate and Mint gin, Treasure Clove gin, Valencian Orange gin, Winter

▲ ***Entrance to City of Aberdeen gin school and distillery.*** (City of Aberdeen)

▼ ***Choosing botanicals at the City of Aberdeen gin school.*** (© City of Aberdeen)

Warmer gin and Mince Pie gin. The range available is regularly changed.

The distillery has become a popular tourist venue in the city. Visitors can participate in a gin tasting masterclass and a distillery tour, and distil a bespoke bottle of gin. The shop is open from midday onwards until late afternoon, Wednesday to Sunday. Tours, classes and experiences must be pre-booked and are mainly held at the weekend.

Other distilleries in the region: Glendornach, Glen Gariach, Glenglassaugh, House of Elrick, Loch Loch, Lone Wolf, Royal Lochnagar

▲ ***Interior of Colonsay distillery.*** (© Isle of Colonsay)

COLONSAY
Tigh na Uruisg
Upper Kilchattan
Isle of Colonsay
PA61 7YR
www.wildthymespirits.com

The distillery was launched in 2016 by a husband and wife team who had moved to the island seeking a quieter, sustainable lifestyle that would contribute to the island economy. The resultant gins are characterised by very other-worldly, faery-like illustrations for the labels, featuring figures such as Alva, a red-haired maiden who is a brownie (small fairy) with supernatural powers. Products include Bramble gin liqueur, Colonsay vodka and gin, and a navy strength version. Ownership of the distillery changed in 2024, when the former Wild Thyme Spirits was taken over by The Island Shop, and renamed Colonsay Distillery.

Visitors can book a distillery tour exploring the gin-making process, finishing with a sampling session. The distillery is open seven days a week.

For longer stays, it is possible to book a 'Gin Lovers' Retreat', staying at the distillery and taking part in a gin tour.

CLYNELISH DISTILLERY
Brora
Sutherland
KW9 6LR
www.malts.com/en-row/distilleries/clynelish

Part of the Diageo group, Clynelish is one of four distilleries involved in the production of Johnny Walker whisky. Clyneish distils a rich Highland malt resulting in a slightly smoky whisky that is rich in flavours of sea spices, florals and honey. It is located on the east coast of Scotland, around one hour north of Inverness on the North Coast 500 route. There has been a distillery on this site since 1819 when the Marquess of Stafford (later the Duke of Sutherland) set out to provide a way of using the barley grown on the estate. It was originally located

▼ ***Clynelish distillery bar.*** (© Clynelish/Diageo)

on what is now the Brora distillery across the road, before closing in 1968 to move to new premises. The existing distillery began production in 1969.

Guided distillery tours are available, varying in content and length, but all include a tasting element. There is also a separate tutored nosing and tasting session providing insights into the history of Clynelish whisky. Other options include a Clynelish whisky weekend combined with a masterclass in making cocktails or an immersive distillery operator-led tour. Pre-booking is recommended. The centre is open seven day a week all year round, but closes slightly earlier between November and March.

There is an on-site bar catering to visitors and offering cocktails, drams, coffees and sharing platters. Products can be purchased from the shop adjacent to the distillery.

Other distilleries in the area: Brora, Dornoch

DALMORE
Alness
Ross and Cromarty
IV17 OUT
www.thedalmore.com

Alexander Matheson founded the distillery in 1839 to produce single malt whisky known as The Dalmore. Control passed to Clan Mackenzie in 1867 and they immediately introduced the iconic emblem of a stag. Since then, all bottles of The Dalmore whisky include a twelve-point royal stag, reflecting the distillery's royal link. The emblem was given to Colin of Kintail, chieftain of Clan Mackenzie when he

Clynelish distillery shop.
(© Clynelish/Diageo)

saved the life of King Alexander III of Scotland from a charging stag. In 1920, part of the distillery was destroyed by an explosion caused by Royal Navy production of deep-sea mines in Cromarty Firth. The resultant legal battle reached the House of Lords before production could recommence. The Dalmore whisky is robust and fruity, resulting from long, complex maturation. The distillery is located on the edge of the Cromarty Firth and is now owned by Whyte & Mackay. Over 4.2 million litres are produced each year. Dalmore is now one of the most famous single malts worldwide, with rare bottles reaching high prices at auction. One sixty-two-year-old bottle reached £25,000. A visitor centre is scheduled for opening in 2025.

Other distilleries in Ross and Cromarty: Badachro, Balblair, Fairytale, Glenmorangie, Singleton of Glen Ord

DALWHINNIE
Dalwhinnie
Inverness-shire
PH19 1AA
www.malts.com/en-gb/distilleries/dalwhinnie

Part of the Diageo group, the Dalwhinnie distillery is located in the beautiful surroundings of the Cairngorm National Park. The name 'Dalwhinnie' comes from a Gaelic world meaning 'meeting place', indicating that this area was once linked to ancient cattle drovers crossing the mountains. It is the highest and coldest working distillery in Scotland, using water sourced from a loch at 2,000 feet above sea level. The resultant whisky contains notes of heather, honey, citrus and vanilla.

Visitors can book guided tours of the distillery, discovering the secrets of its iconic malt. Tours include a tutored tasting, paired with hand-made Scottish highland chocolates. There is an on-site shop.

DEANSTON
Teith Road
Deanston
Doune
Perthshire
FK16 6AG
www.deanstonmalt.com

The distillery buildings began life as a cotton mill in 1785. After nearly 200 years of trading, the cotton mill closed in 1965. A local entrepreneur, Brodie Hepburn, recognised the building's potential with its position along the banks of the River Teith, and within a year had transformed it into a distillery. Hydro-energy fuels the distillery as well as providing the essential water for the distillation process. Production involves a non-chill, no added colour policy. Only traditional methods are used to create the core range plus limited editions.

Deanston whisky is characterised by its smoothness, with notes of honey and heather.

Distillery tours can be booked, also warehouse experiences. Whisky tastings involve a range of selected whiskies. Pre-booking is recommended.

DEERNESS
Newhall
Deerness
Orkney
KW17 2QJ
www.deernessdistillery.com

A self-built distillery in the Orkney Islands, Deerness began trading in 2016, producing gin, vodka, whisky and liqueurs. All products are hand-crafted including the linocut labels, recipes and distilling. It is a family business, located in a very scenic position offering stunning views of Copinsay and the sea. The distillery possesses three Portuguese copper alembic stills. The resulting whisky has a rich, smoky, peated flavour. Several other spirits are produced including the multi-award winning Wild vodka and Scuttled gin. Sea Glass gin is a signature gin inspired by the location, possessing spicy, citrus and pepper flavours.

The site contains a gift shop stocking locally produced jewellery, art and homewares together with Deerness distillery merchandise. Visitors are welcome to see the stills, learn about the distillery and taste the product free of charge. There is no need to book, as visitors are welcomed during trading hours.

DEWAR'S
Aberfeldy
Perthshire
PH15 2EB
www.dewars.com

Located on the outskirts of Aberfeldy, this is the only distillery built by the Dewar family. The company's founder, John Dewar, was born three miles away in the hamlet of Dull. Whisky has been produced here ever since its foundation in 1896, using tall pot stills to create its heather and honey flavoured single malt. In 1896, Dewar's already produced a range of blended whiskies, but wanted to create a single malt. This was the perfect site for the single malt production, with the first such malts becoming available in 1898.

There is a visitor centre on site, offering a range of bookable experiences. These include an Aberfeldy whisky experience complete with tasting sessions, production tours discovering how whisky is blended, creating a bespoke version and tasting old and rare versions. Visitors can also opt for a blender experience and a 'Dram of your Dreams' experience involving a tasting session of the oldest, premium whiskies created by Dewar's. For something different, the 'Hills of Aberfeldy' experience involves a two-night stay in the Pitilie Pods plus special cocktails and private guided tours exploring the distillery's heritage and whisky history.

The heritage museum provides an atmospheric introduction to the history of Dewar's, including period advertisements.

Also available are the John Dewar & Sons Fine Scotch Whisky Emporium, a whisky bar and a whisky lounge/café. Visitors can fill their own bottle from hand-selected casks. Opening hours vary according to season.

DORNOCH
Castle Close
Dornoch
Sutherland
IV25 3SD
www.thompsonbrosdistillers.com

Gin and whisky was initially distilled on this site in 2017 at the Dornoch Castle Hotel, where the company operates a world-leading whisky bar. The first whisky was laid to cask that year. While waiting for the casks to mature, the Dornoch distillery began releasing independent bottlings of rum and whisky as well as its core gin range. Dornoch offers blended variations of Scotch whisky, with its first single malt appearing in 2020. A second distillery was built in Dornoch in 2023/2024 in order to expand the distilling operation. It is sustainable and carbon neutral. A visitor centre and tasting room is being created in the former Dornoch gas works and is anticipated to be available from 2025.

The Dornoch distillery is one of the smallest in Scotland and does not offer any guided tours, however a bottle shop is available at Station Square, Dornoch, selling Thompson Bros and Dornoch distillery products, along with craft beers, organic/biodynamic wines and mixers. The Dornoch Castle Hotel stocks Dornoch products and arranges tastings for different sized groups and budgets.

DUNNET BAY
Dunnet
Caithness
KW14 8XD
www.dunnetbaydistillers.co.uk

A family business, the Dunnet Bay distillery is housed in a purpose-built distillery which was created in 2014. Dunnet Bay has two stills, 'Elizabeth' and 'Margaret', and produces the classic Rock Rose gin. The company seeks to be as environmentally sustainable as possible and is working towards achieving Planet Mark certification. Many of its botanicals are grown on the site and use unusual flavours such as in the Holy Grass vodka. Dunnet Bay now produces a range of award winning gins, vodkas and rums.

Dunnet Bay is located on the North Coast 500 route and the John O'Groats to Land's End tourist route. It is three

▲ ***Mr M. and the Dunnet Bay distillery.*** (© Dunnet Bay)

miles from Dunnet Head, the most northerly point in mainland Britain.

A range of pre-booked tours and experiences are available including distillery tours, tasting sessions, distilling courses and a cocktail workshop. Drivers are asked to bring containers into which samples can be decanted.

There is a shop on site, which also stocks locally produced items as well as Dunnet gin. It is open Monday to Saturday all year round, and on Sundays from May to August.

Dogs are welcome in the shop and garden. Children can take part in the distillery tour and receive a family pack detailing the stories associated with the distillery, but they cannot take part in sampling sessions.

EDRADOUR
Pitlochry
Perthshire
PH16 5JP
www.edrour.com

Eradour produces single malt whisky. It is owned by the Signatory Vintage Scotch Whisky company, and was formerly part of the Pernod Ricard group.

The distillery was founded in 1825 and is situated in a very picturesque area. It now creates over twenty-five different variations of Highland single malt.

Over the years, it has operated distillery tours. These were temporarily stopped due to staffing issues in early 2024, but it is hoped to reintroduce them in due course.

FAIRYTALE
Ardelve
Dornie
Ross-shire
IV40 8DY
www.fairytaledistillery.co.uk

This is a very idiosyncratic small craft distillery based in wooden 'fairy tale' style buildings, together with a bakery and pizzeria designed to blend into the woodland surroundings. Designed to be as sustainable as possible the craft gins are filled into black stone bottles.

Product sampling is available in the distillery shop. There are no distillery tours available.

FETTERCAIRN
Distillery Road
Fettercairn
Laurencekirk
Kincardineshire
AB30 1YB
www.fettercairnwhisky.com

The company was founded by Sir Alexander Ramsay who was one of the first Scottish landowners to campaign for the licensing of Scotch whisky distillation. Fettercairn has been distilling whisky since 1824 when the distillery opened. Five years later the distillery and estate were sold to the Gladstone family. One of their members was the Prime Minister William Gladstone who introduced legislation allowing Scotch to be sold in glass bottles, as well as abolishing taxes on malt and the angels' share. Queen Victoria and Prince Albert visited the local pub, the Ramsay Arms, in 1861 and enjoyed drinks and a meal. A monument commemorating their incognito visit can be seen at the centre of the village.

Fettercairn uses what it claims to be a unique system involving cooling rings which drench the stills in water, thus increasing condensation and enabling only the lightest vapour to rise. This cascading water turns the stills a teal colour, rarely seen in whisky-making. The same colour is used in Fettercairn's packaging and on the bottles. The whisky is golden brown in colour with tropical fruit notes including Madagascan vanilla and red liquorice, giving it a spiced element. There is a core collection alongside limited releases, rare and aged versions, plus a warehouse. The bottles bear an iconic unicorn emblem.

Fettercairn now has a refurbished visitor centre. Distillery tours complete with sampling of drams are available throughout spring, summer and autumn. Booking is recommended.

GATEHOUSE GIN

Gleneagles
Auchterarder
Perthshire
PH3 1PN
www.gatehousegin.co.uk

Gatehouse gin was launched in 2019. It is a joint venture between Tony Reeman-Clark, founder of Strathearn distillery, and Wyndham Duchally Country Estate. Ingredients from the botanical garden and orchard belonging to the Wyndham Duchally Country Estate are used in the signature Gatehouse gin, which has flavours of apple, gooseberry and rosehip. It is distilled in 100-litre alembic stills.

Wyndham Duchally Country Estate comprises a country house and luxurious lodges. It was originally built for the Monteath family in 1838. Pre-booked gin tasting experiences and a session creating a bespoke gin are available at the distillery. There is also a cocktail masterclass.

GLENCADAM

Smithfield Road
Brechin
Angus
DD9 7PA
www.glencadamwhisky.com

Founded in 1825, production methods at Glencadam have hardly changed over the years. It still uses traditional and hand-crafted processes. The reintroduction of a waterwheel in 2021 linked back to the original energy methods of 200 years ago. Glencadam is owned by Angus Dundee plc. It produces a malt whisky, with the remainder of the distillation used in Angus Dundee blended whiskies or sold to independent bottlers. Whiskies are bottled at 46%. They are not chill-filtered or coloured.

There is an on-site shop. A visitor centre is being constructed and distillery tours are planned. Visitors should contact the company regarding availability.

GLENDRONACH
Forgue
Huntly
Aberdeenshire
AB54 6DB
www.glendronachdistillery.com

Glendronach was one of the first licensed Scottish distilleries, having been founded in 1826. By the 1860s it had become one of the largest duty-paying distilleries in the Highlands. Glendronach pioneered the use of sherry cask maturation, giving the whisky exceptional depth of flavour. In 1960, William Teacher & Sons acquired the business and the number of stills was expanded to four. The site was mothballed in 1996 and reopened in 2002. Three years later, Glendronach's parent company Allied Distillers was taken over by Pernod Ricard. The distillery operation came under the control of Chivas Brothers. Changes were quickly made, converting the stills to steam heating rather than the traditional coal fire. In 2008, ownership of Glendronach changed again, this time to the privately owned BenRiach Distillery Company. Production increased and the distillery's stature in the industry rose, leading to it being awarded the prestigious title of Global Whisky Distiller of 2015. The following year, the company was taken over by the Brown-Forman Corporation.

Visitors are welcomed all year round. Guided tours are available, including a visit to one of the warehouses and a tasting session. Booking is recommended. Along with the visitor centre, the site also has a gift shop and tasting bar.

GLEN GARIOCH
Distillery Road
Oldmeldrum
Inverurie
Aberdeenshire
AB51 0ES
www.glengarioch.com

Glen Garioch was founded in 1797, with ownership changing between various companies over the years. It is now operated by Morrison Bowmore Distillers, owned by Beam Suntory. The company initiated an innovative waste–heat recovery system in 1980 called the Greenhouse Project, which utilised waste heat for the malt kiln, and warmed two acres of glashouses and polytunnels. As a result, the distillery became famous for its tomatoes, peppers, aubergines and cucumbers as well as its whisky. The project was discontinued in 1993. From 1997, Glen Garioch whisky has been unpeated, and it produces single malts, which have a creamy texture and a honey flavour. The site was reopened to the public in 2022 following a £6 million refurbishment that included the introduction of direct fired distillation designed to cut its carbon footprint by 15%.

The Glen Garioch visitor centre is open throughout the year. The on-site shop sells a wide range of Glen Garioch merchandise. A variety of visitor experiences and guided tours can be booked including whisky and cheese tastings, masterclasses, 'Legends of the Garioch Valley', 'Bottle Your Own Highland Single Malt' and tours of the production facilities.

GLENGLASSAUGH
Portsoy
Aberdeenshire
A45 2SQ
www.glenglassaugh.com

Enjoy beautiful views over Sandend Bay, watching gannets and dolphins when visiting the Glenglassaugh distillery. In 1875, James Moir founded the distillery on the banks of the Glassaugh Burn. It was mothballed in the 1980s before production restarted in 2008. In 2013, it was sold to the BenRiach distillery, and subsequently sold together with BenRiach and Glendronach to Brown-Forman. Glenglassaugh produces single malt Scotch whisky with flavour profiles reflecting its coastal location. In 2023, a rare bottle of Glenglassaugh raised £37,500 at auction in aid of a charity for disadvantaged young people.

A limited number of private and exclusive pre-booked distillery tours are available. They include an introduction to the history of the area, as well as exploring the traditional distilling methods in use. Bespoke experiences can be arranged.

GLENMORANGIE
Tain
Ross-shire
IV19 1PZ
www.glenmorangie.com

Founded in 1843 by William Matheson, Glenmorangie is now owned by the Glenmorangie Company Ltd, part of the Diageo group. The Gaelic name means 'valley of tranquillity'.

The main product is single malt whisky which is produced using copper stills that are the tallest in Scotland, measuring 5.14 metres high. The sheer height of these stills led Glenmorangie to adopt the giraffe as its mascot, since the giraffe is the same height. A key element in the complex flavours of the whisky is the water from the Tarlogie Springs on the site, which are rich in minerals. In order to ensure the continued purity of this water, Glenmorangie owns all the forests around the water source.

Tours and tastings are available. These include guided tours of the distillery, and experimental tasting sessions where innovative expressions can be tried. There is also a 'Wonder' tour available during the high summer season which focuses on attempts to create new flavours complemented by cheese and fine

▲ ***Glenmorangie distillery.*** (© Glenmorangie)

▲ ***The tall stills at Glenmorangie.*** (© Glenmorangie)

chocolate pairings. Visitors can also stay at the distillery's boutique hotel, Glenmorangie House, complete with outdoor seating areas, and access to a rocky shoreline and walled garden. There is a communal dining table at Glenmorangie offering a continually changing range of lunch and dinner menus.

GLENTURRET
The Hosh
Crieff
Perthshire
PH7 4HA
www.theglenturret.com

Glenturret is Scotland's oldest working distillery, creating only hand-crafted malt whisky. It possesses the only remaining hand-operated mash tun in the country. Distilling was recorded here in 1763. 'Glenturret' means 'land of the rushing stream' and it is this water that is used in the distillation process. By 1890, whisky was being exported to Australia, the USA and South Africa. The site was mothballed for over thirty years, reopening in 1957 under new ownership.

In 1980, one of Scotland's first distillery visitor centres was launched at Glenturret capitalising on the

▲ ***The Glenturret distillery.*** (© **Glenturret**)

▼ ***Glenturret open day.*** (© Glenturret)

growing interest in whisky tourism. The centre quickly gained popularity and in 1991 welcomed its millionth visitor. Glenturret is now owned by a joint venture led by the Lalique Group and Swiss-American Hansjörg Wyss. Also on site is the Aberturret Estate House, the distillery brand home which can be booked for exclusive use and events.

Visitors can enjoy a range of distillery tours, sample a Lalique whisky flight or create a bespoke whisky. The distillery has a gift shop offering Glenturret merchandise and locally crafted gifts, as well as a café housed in the former maltings store. Unique to Glenturret is its two Michelin-starred restaurant, the first fine dining restaurant of its kind in a distillery.

For visitors seeking a more immersive experience, the 'Gastronomic Stay' includes a multi-course dinner reservation at the Glenturret Lalique Restaurant and an overnight stay at the Aberturret Estate House.

GREAT GLEN
Loch Ness Centre
Drumnadrochit
Inverness
IV63 6TU
www.greatglendistillery.co.uk
www.lochnesscentre.com

Established in 2020, this is a small craft distillery on the bank of Loch Ness, which sets out to reflect the beauty of the Great Glen that surrounds the lake. Distilling has a long history in this area, as just to the north is the village of Abriachan where, centuries ago, the legendary 'King of Smugglers' Donald Fraser illegally distilled highly prized whisky.

Great Glen creates its spirits using only locally sourced ingredients such as hand-picked wild Scottish heather from and local Highland water. Among its produce is Great Glen Premium Scottish pink gin and Caledonian Canal gin. The bottle labels contain two separate designs, as the back of the label when seen through the bottle has another image – for example, the Caledonian Canal gin label shows a labelled map of the canal while the Great Glen gin has detailed maps of the Glen.

The distillery forms part of the Loch Ness Centre, enabling visitors to stay on site in the hotel, and take advantage of other facilities such as cruises involving sonar to scan the waters of the loch. Visitors can also enjoy gin tasting sessions and visit the distillery.

HIGHLAND PARK
Holm Road
Kirkwall
Orkney
KW15 1SU
www.highlandparkwhisky.com

Located high above the town of Kirkwall, the distillery offers wonderful views of the coast. Whisky has been produced at this site since 1798 when a local butcher and church officer distilled whisky illegally, smuggling it to his clients. An official licence was granted in 1826 to distil whisky. Only traditional methods are used, just as when whisky was first produced here. The resultant beverage is based on local flavours and tastes. There are two pagoda-topped kilns and twenty-three warehouses. The youngest kiln is over 100 years old. Fuel for the kilns comes from local peat hand-cut on Hobbister Moor. All the whisky is matured in sherry-seasoned oak casks, and results in a core range of single malts plus special limited editions.

There is a visitor centre offering a variety of guided tours including 'Orcadian Vintages', and tasting sessions. Highland Park has a shop in Kirkwall where visitors can also learn about the Viking heritage of the Orkneys.

▲ ***Gin tour, House of Elrick.*** (© House of Elrick)

HOUSE OF ELRICK
Elrick House
Newmachar
Aberdeenshire
AB21 7PY
www.houseofelrick.co.uk

The distillery forms part of the historic eighteenth-century Elrick Estate which is being brought back to life by Stuart Ingram, who is restoring the landscape and house with the aid of crowdfunding initiatives. He has appeared on *Dragons' Den* and secured an investment from Peter Jones, but later decided against taking up the offer.

Founded in 2018, the distillery has a copper pot still and a state of the art bottling line. Gin is produced in small batches of just 600 bottles to provide complete traceability, quality and integrity of the spirit. Local farmers and suppliers provide the raw materials for each batch of spirit. Apart from gin, House of Elrick also produces a range of rums and rum liquors, reflecting the area's rum smuggling history. Typical

▲ ***House of Elrick gin distilling.*** (© House of Elrick)

flavourings used in the range of spirits include spices, blood orange, heather, rose and sweet fennel.

Pre-booked tours are available during weekdays only. Each tour is introduced with the story of the Elrick Estate, the creation of the signature gin, a tour of the distillery and an opportunity to sample three of the premium gins.

ICE AND FIRE
Smerral
Latheronwheel
Caithness
www.iceandfiredistillery.com

Ice and Fire was set up by a family of Highland crofters as a way of supplementing their crofting income. It produces three spirits: Caithness gin, Crofter's Tears gin and Caithness Raiders rum. An artisan distillery, every batch of spirits is hand-crafted in small quantities using 200-litre Hoga stills. The brand and labels reflect the local heritage, including the famed Northern Lights which can frequently be seen illuminating the skies in winter.

The distillery offers the opportunity to spend a weekend at the Crofter's Retreat on the site – a four-bedroom country house with scenic views. As part of the weekend, it is possible to take a masterclass in blending your own signature gin, possibly foraging for local botanicals. The session also includes exploring the making of Caithness and Crofter's Tears gin, plus cutting the heads, hearts and tails from a batch of gin.

ISLE OF BARRA
Castlebay
Isle of Barra
HS9 5XF
www.isleofbarradistillers.com

A family distillery set up in 2017, it is the first legal distillery to be created on the island. Inspiration is provided by the local environment – for example, its Barra Atlantic gin is distilled using locally harvested carrageen seaweed.

Members of the public can buy Isle of Barra products from the distillery shop but there are no distillery tours available.

ISLE OF CUMBRAE
11 Guildford Street
Milport
North Ayrshire
KA28 OAE
www.isleofcumbrae-distillers.com

Launched by an all-female distilling team brought together by a love of gin in 2019, the ownership has evolved over time. In 2024, several of the original founders retired, leaving the company in the ownership of Caroline and Struan Fraser.

The company's first gins were launched in 2020, and that same year

▲ ***Isle of Cumbrae distillery shop.*** (© ***Isle of Cumbrae***)

▼ ***'Maura', Isle of Cumbrae's still.*** (© Isle of Cumbrae)

won major awards at the Gin Masters and the International Wine and Spirit Competition (IWSC), as well as being a finalist in the Scottish Gin Awards. The gins are designed to celebrate Scottish history, coastal waters and harbour towns like Milport. All the bottles have been carefully chosen to encourage people to repurpose them around the home. Typical gins include the Croc Rock gin and Nostalgin.

There are a variety of tours and tastings available. The gin distillery tours are designed to bring to life the history of gin, the role women played in gin and the colourful smuggling history of the Clyde, along with the story of Cumbrae and methods of gin distilling, plus sampling of Cumbrae gins.

ISLE OF HARRIS

Tarbert
Isle of Harris
Outer Hebrides
www.harrisdistillery.com

Distilling spirits on the island was a common practice before the 1840s, when the Pabbay clearances put an end to the tradition. Founded in 2015, the distillery was seen as a way of providing employment for young people, encouraging them to stay on the island rather than having to move to the mainland to find work. The company has grown steadily and now employs over fifty people and is proving to be a catalyst for change in the local community.

▼ ***Isle of Harris distillery.*** (© Isle of Harris)

The Isle of Harris distillery produces the Hearach, a single malt whisky which is non-chill filtered and free from artificial colouring. Water on the island is said to be the softest of any Scottish distillery, possessing very low levels of sodium and chlorine. The prevailing Gulf Stream currents ensure that seasonal temperatures are very stable, thus benefiting maturation. Isle of Harris gin is distilled in a small copper still, using locally harvested sugar kelp seaweed from the sea lochs as the key ingredient, stressing the gin's maritime nature. It is distilled in small batches using traditional techniques.

Visitors are welcome at the distillery and its own site shop. Samplings and tastings are available, along with opportunities to enjoy a coffee or a cocktail.

JURA WHISKY
Craighouse
Isle of Jura
PA60 7XT
www.jurawhisky.com

Located on the Inner Hebridean island of Jura, the distillery is operated by Whyte & Mackay. It was founded in 1810 but fell into disrepair from 1901 onwards. In 1963, local landowners rebuilt the distillery and began distilling spirits. The site now distils a range of single malt Scotch whiskies include a fourteen-year-old American rye cask whisky. Jura Whisky's iconic bottle reflects the perils of the treacherous waters surrounding the island, which include the world's third largest whirlpool, the Corryvreckan. According to the Royal Navy these are some of the most treacherous waters to be found around the British coast. Jura created its iconic bottle to withstand the perils of such dangerous waters. It produces a range of single malt Scotch whiskies, including the Signature, Expressions and Vintage selections.

Access to the Isle of Jura is via two ferries, one from the Isle of Islay and the other from Kennacraig on the mainland to Islay.

Weekday distillery tours are available but must be booked in advance. Each tour includes a sampling session. Jura Whisky Expressions and related merchandise can be purchased from the visitor centre. It is open weekdays all year round, and closed at weekends during the winter. In the summer, the distillery is closed on Sundays. There is an on-site shop.

ISLE OF RAASAY
Borodale House
Kyle
Isle of Raasay
IV40 8PB
www.raasaydistillery.com

Launched in 2014, the distillery is the first to be operated legally on the island. It is owned by R&B Distillers and is located in a landmark building. It produces both Isle of Raasay single malt whisky (peated and unpeated versions) and Isle of Raasay gin. The whisky is matured in ex-rye whiskey, fresh chinkapin oak and former Bordeaux red wine casks. The gin is described as dry, zesty and smooth, using local juniper double distilled spirit, and is bottled in eye-catching containers reflecting the island's geology. The water used in the production process comes from a Celtic Iron Age well which has a high mineral content.

Immersive distillery tours can be booked. These include a whisky, gin and chocolate tour and tasting experience and a dunnage cask warehouse tour.

Access to Raasay is via a short ferry trip from the Isle of Skye. Accommodation is available at the four-star boutique hotel on site. The Isle of Raasay is the only Scottish distillery in which visitors can stay overnight in the same building as a working distillery. There is also a restaurant in Borodale House. Anyone looking for a special weekend away can opt for a whisky retreat involving a hotel stay with a distillery production and bottling warehouse tour, and a paired whisky and chocolate tasting.

ISLE OF SKYE
The Distillery at Hillfoot
Viewfield Road
Portree
Isle of Skye
IV51 9ES
www.isleofskyedistillers.com

An independent family-run craft spirit distillery, Isle of Skye produces Misty Isle gin and Misty Isle vodka using locally foraged botanicals and water from the Storr Lochs. There are plans to extend the distillery to provide whisky production and a spiced rum range.

There are no visitor facilities at the distillery, but there is a shop located in the centre of Portrae offering free Misty Isle gin tastings. Samples of whisky can be provided for a small fee. Guest tasting sessions are often provided, and these are announced on the Isle of Skye Distillers Instagram and Facebook pages. In addition to the gin and whisky ranges, the shop sells branded merchandise and local arts and crafts. A second shop is located in Breaknish Old Post Office and also offers gin and whisky tastings.

ISLE OF TIREE
1A West
Hynish
Isle of Tiree
PA77 6UF
www.tyreegin.com

Over 200 years ago, the Isle of Tiree was home to over fifty distilleries despite being just twelve miles long and three miles wide. In 1802, the Duke of Argyll banned distilling on the island due to the intemperance of the islanders. Now there is just one distillery, founded in 2012. It is an independent, locally-owned business designed to raise the island's profile. At its launch during

▲ ***Isle of Tiree distillery.*** (© Malcolm Steel, Isle of Tiree)

the Tiree Homecoming, the entire 230 bottles of its first malt were totally sold out. A small distillery, it produces single malt Scotch whisky, single grain rye-based Scotch whisky as well as two varieties of gin. The gin uses local botanicals dried on rocks, naturally by the sun. Tyree gin uses a historical form of spelling for the island. The whisky is not peated as there are no supplies on the island. According to reports, the sheer amount of illicit distilling that once took place on Tiree caused peat supplies to run out.

There is a distillery shop along with a visitor centre open during the summer season. The distillery offers tours exploring the island's distilling heritage, the creation of Tyree gin and Hebridean pink gin and also its recently established whisky production, together with a cocktail evening experience. Gin sampling is provided either on site or as miniatures for drivers to take away.

LAGG
Kilmory
Isle of Arran
KA27 8PG
www.laggwhisky.com

Historically, Arran communities used to create 'Arran Waters' spirit using illicit home-made stills which was smuggled from Lagg and sold on the mainland. The Lagg distillery opened in 2019 complete with a visitor centre. Architecturally it is spectacular since it is designed to echo the contours

Lagg distillery, Isle of Arran. (© Lagg)

of Arran as seen from Ailsa Crag, and is covered with a sedum roof. The distillery produces a peat-smoked single malt whisky. There is an on-site café. Visitors can order a whisky flight of three or four drams.

The Arran Whisky Festival combining 'malt and music' is held annually. Tickets must be pre-booked. Visitors can book tours of the distillery showing how the company is using traditional methods to create a contemporary-style peated whisky. Several variations of these tours are available varying in length and with differing amounts of samples. Takeaway samples are available for drivers.

Other tours include a festive exclusive 'Winter Favourites' tasting session, an 'Inaugural Releases' tasting, 'Secrets from the Lagg Vault', whisky and chocolate pairings involving locally made chocolate, and a historically-based experience focusing on 'Arran Water Tales and Drams', which features the misadventures of Arran's smuggling past.

Tours should be booked online.

LOCHRANZA
Lochranza
Isle of Arran
KA27 8HJ
www.arranwhisky.com

Lochranza is the second of Arran's distilleries and is located on the north side of the island. The setting

Lochranza distillery. (© Lochranza)

is very different to that of Lagg, since mountain peaks overshadow the Lochranza distillery. Arran has a long history of small-scale distilling, but when faced with demands of quantity over quality, distillers were unable to compete with the larger mainland distilleries. In 1993, a decision was taken to restart distilling on Arran, and a location at Lochranza was chosen due to the high quality of the water in the area. Initial building works had to be temporarily halted when eagle owls arrived to nest high in the hills above Lochranza. Since then, the eagle owls have returned many times to the area when nesting, and can frequently been seen flying high above the distillery. The distillery opened in 1995, with the visitor centre being opened by HM Queen Elizabeth the same year. The first legal dram of Arran single malt Scotch whisky was served in 1998, with the first commercially available Arran Malt ten-year-old becoming available in 2006. Other expressions have been released since then, including a peated 'Machrie Moor' version.

Tasting sessions and food service are available at the Lochranza distillery café located in the visitor centre. Driver's drams can be provided for those unable to sample whiskies during the visit. A variety of guided tours can be booked including the 'Arran Malt Experience' distillery tour and a Lochranza selected tasting. All experiences need to be pre-booked.

LONE WOLF
Balmacassie Commercial Park
Ellon
Aberdeenshire
AB41 8BX
www.lonewolfgin.com

Lone Wolf is owned by BrewDog, which was founded in 2007, initially as a craft beer brewer. Since then the company has grown significantly, and moved into the production of other alcoholic beverages. The distillery produces gin, vodka, rum and whisky. The Lone Wolf brand of gin was first produced in 2016 and possesses flavours of grapefruit and lavender, plus a Scottish character from pine needles. It has since developed other variations on the Lone Wolf theme such as Cloudy Lemon, using Sicilian lemon peel, and Cactus and Lime. The site includes three large whisky stills, a column still for vodka production, a 20-metre high rectification column gin still plus a 50-litre still for experimentation. Double distillation is standard, but triple distillation is possible. Whisky is matured in ex-bourbon barrels, or in sherry and port wine casks.

Tours and tastings can be booked online. Visitors can see the original brewhouse, plus the Lone Wolf distillery.

LOST LOCH SPIRITS
Deeside Activity Park
Dess
Aboyne
Aberdeenshire
AB34 5BD
www.lostlochspirits.com

Set in the heart of Royal Deeside, Lost Loch is located on the banks of the now drained Loch Auchlossan (the 'Lost Loch'). It is an independent company using only local ingredients, creating brands like eeNoo gin, Murmichan absinthe and Haroosh whisky liqueur. EeNoo is distilled with Royal Deeside honey and a variety of botanicals plus heather flowers, rosehips and berries grown in Aberdeenshire. Haroosh is something very different when it comes to liqueurs. Lost Loch use a blend of Scottish whiskies together with local blackberries and Deeside honey, sealed with beeswax. Each bottle contains at least fifty berries while

▲ ***Interior of Lost Loch distillery and gin school.*** (© Lost Loch)

the bees travel 4,500 miles to collect enough honey for each bottle. As well as producing its own multi-award winning spirits, it undertakes contract distilling, specialising in working with innovators, start-up brands and entrepreneurs, using its knowledge and equipment to get ideas into a bottle, creating something bespoke or off the shelf. Many of its contract products have won awards.

Pre-booked micro-tours of the distillery are available, along with tasting sessions and creating bespoke spirits in the Lost Loch spirits school. Tours include hearing stories about the unique products such as Scotland's first absinthe, Murmichan, the 'Wall of Botanicals' and distilling methods.

LUSSA GIN
The Stables
Ardlussa
Isle of Jura
PA60 7XW
www.lussagin.com

Lussa gin is produced using locally-grown botanicals such as lemon thyme, roses, coriander, elderflower, lemon balm and lime flowers. The company is owned by a group of local people, who

Lussa gin. (© Lussa)

came together due to their love of the island and its environment.

Pre-booked guided tours of the distillery are available.

NC'NEAN
Drimnin
By Lochaline
Argyll
PA80 5XZ
www.ncnean.com

Nc'nean is an independent, organic whisky distillery creating experimental spirits and pioneering sustainable production. Distilling began in 2017, with the first bottling in 2020. Based on the Morven peninsula on the wild west coast of Scotland, Nc'nean produces a light and fruity style of single malt which can exist in harmony with the earth. B Corp certified, Nc'nean uses only organic Scottish barley in a distillery powered entirely by renewable energy.

The whisky is bottled in a 100% recycled clear glass bottle and 99.97% of waste is diverted from landfill. As of 2021, Nc'nean became the first whisky distillery in the UK to be verified as having net zero carbon emissions for scopes 1 and 3.

▲ ***Nc'nean distillery from above.*** (© Nc'nean)

▼ ***Nc'nean distillery in springtime.*** (© Nc'Nean)

In addition to its range of whiskies, Nc'nean produces a botanical spirit which is distilled with a combination of classic gin botanicals and local Scottish plants. The barley spirit used adds a malty, fruity undertone. In 2024, the company launched a bottle return scheme, enabling people to return empty bottles to the distillery to be reused.

Guided tours are available but must be pre-booked. In addition to the distillery tour, visitors can opt for a sustainability tour which showcases the distillery's pioneering efforts in sustainable whisky production. Throughout the summer months visitors can reach the distillery by water taxi from Tobermory. There are also two moorings located a short walk from the distillery and its shop, which stocks a range of Nc'nean products as well as some local gifts and art. The shop is open daily during the week.

NORTH POINT

Forss Business and Energy Park
Near Thurso
Caithness
KW14 7UZ
www.northpointdistillery.com

Founded in 2020 as an independent business, North Point distils premium quality spirits, including Dalclagie single malt whisky, Crosskirk Bay gin, North Point spiced rum and North Point Pilot rum. All the spirits are created in small batches, designed to be as environmentally friendly as possible, and have won many awards, nationally and internationally.

Overlooking the Pentland Forth, the distillery is unusual in that the site was originally built as a US Navy radio listening site for NATO during

North Point distillery. (© North Point)

the Cold War. A cairn bears witness to the American link, as it was built on their departure, bearing the words 'Supporting the fleet was our mission, world peace was our goal.' There are many other historical links with stories of smugglers in Crosskirk Bay and a prehistoric cairn said to be the first *broch* (a prehistoric circular stone tower) ever built.

Guided tours are available all year round with sampling sessions included. Tours must be pre-booked. Private cocktail evenings can be arranged for

North Point distillery shop. (© North Point)

North Uist distillery. (© North Uist)

small groups. There is also an on-site shop showcasing the spirits and locally crafted goods.

NORTH UIST
Baile nan Cailleach
Nunton Steadings
Benbecula
Outer Hebrides
HS7 5LU
www.northuistdistillery.com

Owned by an islander family, North Uist distillery was founded in 2019. Located at Nunton Steading, the site dates back to the 1300s. Its first alcoholic beverage was Downpour Scottish dry gin, flavoured with the blossoms of wild Hebridean heather. It has since expanded into other Downpour editions such as Sloe and Bramble, and has now moved into whisky distilling. The first whisky was produced in 2024.

Whisky distilling has a long history on the island, and for most of the time was the result of illicit stills. North Uist's whisky will use locally bere barley (a Scottish six-row barley) grown by local crofters.

North Uist occupies a historic eighteenth-century steading know as Nunton Steading. It was once a nunnery, and according to legend it was here that Bonnie Prince Charlie's escape was planned after the Battle of Culloden.

The company is intent on restoring historic whisky and gin distilling on the island. As part of the building restoration, the intention is to reinstate traditions such as the bell at

North Uist gin. (© North Uist)

Nunton, which was rung out whenever important events occurred. It will ring again when the first drop of Nunton whisky is drunk at the steading building, marking the return of whisky distilling.

North Uist distillery welcomes visitors to its shop. Cocktail masterclasses can be booked, along with pre-booked guided gin and whisky tours and tasting sessions, plus a walk-through tour of the Nunton Steading site. Visitors can also relax in the Island Life Bar or, when weather allows, in the courtyard. North Uist runs a barter system for visitors – provide botanicals (heather, pepper dulse, wild thyme or brambles) in return for gin.

OBAN WHISKY
Stafford Street
Oban
Argyll
PA34 5NH
www.obanwhisky.com

Nestling under the steep cliff overlooking Oban is one of the smallest and oldest Scotch whisky distilleries. It occupies exactly the same location as when distilling first began here, and it has never expanded in size. Distilling began in 1793, producing Cowbell ale as well as whisky. Ownership has changed several times over the years. It produces several varieties of single malt Scotch whisky using two stills, valuing craftsmanship over speed. These malts include Little Bay, which has a dark chocolate finish and notes of Christmas pudding, citrus and spice.

Guided tours of the distillery can be booked, along with tutored tasting sessions.

OLD PULTENEY
Huddart Street
Wick
Caithness
KW1 5BA
www.oldpulteney.com

Owned by Inver House Distillers, the Old Pulteney Distillery is one of the northernmost distilleries in the country. Founded in 1826, the ingredients had to be brought in by sea. The resultant whisky was also shipped out by sea using the services of herring fishermen (who also worked in the distillery). Unusually the port became 'dry' in 1920 under the terms of the Temperance (Scotland) Act resulting in pubs being boarded up and the distillery eventually closing. It was not until 1951 that production resumed. It now produces hand-crafted Old Pulteney single malt whisky, creating around 900,000 litres a year. Aged in American oak casks, the whisky incorporates a faint salty flavour reflecting its Caithness coast origins. All the water used in the whisky production comes from Loch Hempriggs, using a lade designed by the famous engineer Thomas Telford in 1807.

A range of tours and experiences are available most of the year at Pulteney's visitor centre, including opportunities to taste various whiskies. Pre-booking is recommended.

ORKNEY DISTILLING
Ayre Road
Kirkwall
Isle of Orkney
KW15 1QX
www.orkneydistilling.com

Orkney gin is based very much on the island's heritage, inspired by its past and seeking to develop a business that is part of the community. The gin is hand-crafted in small batches using traditional copper stills. All the ingredients, including barley, are locally sourced. In 2024, the company gained a licence to distil Orkney single malt Scotch whisky and is now in the process of creating its whisky and rum.

The range includes Kirkjuvagr Orkney gin, named after the Norse seafarers who would sail into the bay to trade at Kirkjuvagr, the town that eventually developed into Kirkwall, the Orkney capital. An essential ingredient in Kirkjuvagr gin is a variety of the angelica herb, brought to the islands by the Norsemen and still growing in the wild today.

The distillery is open seven days a week. Guided tours can be pre-booked,

The Orkney distillery. (© Orkney Distilling)

exploring the process of distillation plus gin sampling. Options are available for designated drivers and under 18s to enjoy the tour alcohol-free.

PERTH
George Inn Lane
Tay Street
Perthshire
PH1 5LG
www.perthdistillery.co.uk

The Perth distillery is a small independent distillery creating small-batch drinks inspired by the City of Perth. These include Perth Pink, Blood Orange liqueur gin and a spiced winter liqueur gin. All the gins are hand-crafted in copper alembic stills.

A range of pre-booked tours, tastings and gin experiences is available at the distillery. Typically these include a welcome gin and tonic on arrival, an exploration of the history of gin, a tour of the distillery and gin palace, plus a sampling session. There is a shop on site.

PERSIE DISTILLERY
Old Military Road (A93)
Bridge of Cally
Perthshire
PH10 7LQ
www.persiedistillery.com

A gin distillery, Persie creates hand-crafted beverages on the site of the former Persie Hotel, Glenshee. The husband and wife team behind the business created the world's first touring gin club in 2013, before opening the Persie distillery in 2016. This is a distillery with a purpose, dedicated to raising

Persie distillery. (© Persie)

▲ ***Visitors to the Persie distillery.*** (© Persie)

money for animal welfare. It is dedicated charity partner is PADS (Perthshire Abandoned Dogs Society). There are three 'dog gins' with each recipe carefully created to reflect a breed of dog, with sales from each bottle raising funds for PADS. Labrador gin is mellow, soft in the mouth and warming with juniper and eucalyptus; Spaniel gin is lively and spicy, featuring nutmeg and cinnamon; and Dachshund gin is like the breed – a sweet but sharp citrus liqueur. There is also a vodka available called Pusscat, which helps support the Edinburgh Dog and Cat Home.

The distillery is open to visitors all year round, and is dog friendly. All spirits are hand-crafted on site with tastings and tours available every day.

PIXEL SPIRITS
Old Ferry Road
North Ballachulish
Fort William
Inverness-shire
PH33 6SA
www.pixelspiritsltd.co.uk

A gin, vodka and rum distillery located in the grounds of the Loch Leven Hotel near Glencoe, Pixel Spirits is a family-owned artisan distillery housed in a traditional A-frame barn. All the spirits distilled here are small batches, labelled

▲ **Pixel Spirits.** (© Pixel Spirits/Loch Leven)

▼ **Loch Leven Hotel.** (© Pixel Spirits/Loch Leven)

and bottled on site by hand. There are two stills – one 100 litre and the other 500 litre. Pixel produces signature ranges such as the Devil's Staircase, named after a nearby mountain ascent, part of the West Highland Way. There is also an artisan range, for example Chanterelle gin – which has a chanterelle mushroom influence – Scottish golden rum and seasonal produce.

Visitors can book sessions at the gin school and the rum school. Pixel was one of the first Scottish distilleries to offer distillation courses, and visitors can use copper pot mini-stills to create a bespoke gin or rum. A tour of the distillery is included in the session. Alternatively, visitors can book a gin tasting and distillery tour. Accommodation is available at the hotel on site.

PRABAN NA LINNE
Gaelic Whiskies and Gaelic Gins
Eilean Iarmain
Sleat
Isle of Skye
IV43 8QR
www.gaelicwhisky.com

Praban Na Linne is small, independent, artisan distiller located on the Isle of Skye. Founded in 1976 by Scottish entrepreneur Sir Iain Noble, it produces a premium range of blended whisky possessing a high malt content that has been aged in sherry casks. The range was designed to reflect the linguistic and cultural heritage of the Hebridean islands while supplying work for local people. The Gaelic gins, known as *uisge lusach* (herbaceous water), have a similar approach, and are distilled in a small copper pot still reminiscent of the stills once used to distil illicit whisky.

There are no tours of the distillery available, but there is a shop on site with the opportunity to taste the whisky and gin.

ROYAL LOCHNAGAR
Crathie
Ballater
Aberdeenshire
AB35 5TB
www.malts.com/en-row/distilleries/royal-lochnagar

Beautifully located on the banks of the River Dee close to Balmoral Castle, the Royal Lochnagar distillery produces an exclusive range of golden-coloured single malt whiskies. The company gained its name following a visit by Queen Victoria and Prince Albert in 1848. It is a small distillery possessing traditional pagoda kiln heads and open mash tuns. Flavours are described as delicate, fruity, woody and light toffee.

Booking tours in advance is recommended, as they are very popular. The visitor centre offers a selection of tours including guided tours of the distillery, tutor tasting and a limited edition expressions tour.

SCAPA
St Ola
Kirkwall
Isle of Orkney
KW15 1SE
www.scapawhisky.com

The Scapa distillery is located on the banks of the Scapa Flow, renowned as one of the most historic stretches of water in the UK. The whisky is matured in first-fill American oak casks and is smooth and creamy, possessing floral notes. No peat is used in drying the malt, allowing the sweet and tropical flavours of Scapa to emerge.

Tours of the distillery and warehouses can be booked, along with tasting sessions. The site has a stunning tasting room with views across the coastline. It includes many elements linked to the area's history, including a helmet over 100 years old, in a style used by the British Navy until the 1970s. Much of the stonework has been reused and repurposed from around the island while the ceiling is crafted in the style of a typical fishing boat interior. Bespoke tastings can be arranged.

SHETLAND
Saxa Vord
Unst
Shetland Islands
www.shetlandreel.com

This is the most northerly distillery in the UK, and is only accessible from the Shetland mainland by two ferry journeys, via the island of Yell. A locally-owned business, it aims to produce high quality products, as well as being an award winning tourist resort complete with all year round self-catering accommodation, a seasonal hotel and a bar/restaurant. The onsite malt whisky company produces single cask, single malt whiskies, as well as small-batch gin ranges. These include Shetland Reel Ocean Sent gin, Gin Bean, Up Helly Aa gin, Wild Fire gin and Filska gin.

▲ ***Shetland Saxa Vord distillery display.*** (© Shetland Distillery Company)

Visitors can book guided tasting sessions, held daily between Tuesday and Saturday.

SINGLETON OF GLEN ORD
Muir of Ord
Easter Ross
IV6 7UJ
www.malts.com/en-row/distilleries/the-singleton-of-glen-ord

Located in the heart of the Black Isle, near Inverness, the Glen Ord distillery uses American bourbon and European sherry casks to mature its single malt Scotch whisky. It was originally built in 1897 and was the seventh distillery to be constructed in Dufftown. Distribution nationwide was made possible by the distillery's private railway. By 1902, its whisky had become popular at the court of King Edward VII. The slow fermentation and distillation process results in a whisky with a smooth, rich flavour.

▲ ***The Singleton, Glen Ord distillery.*** (© Glen Ord/Diageo)

▼ ***The Singleton Bar at Glen Ord.*** (© Glen Ord/Diageo)

Visitor experiences include whisky and food pairing, guided distillery tours, tasting sessions and 'Singleton Sessions' combining whisky, cocktails and seasonal platters with music. Occasional special experiences are available such as a 'Silent Season' cask draw and an exclusive tasting as part of an evolution of whisky session. There is an onsite shop, bar and social space offering locally sourced food. Advance booking of tours and experiences in advance is recommended.

TALISKER
Carbost
Isle of Skye
IV47 8SR
www.malts.com/en-gb/distilleries/talisker

Located on the Isle of Skye, the Talisker distillery is ideally sited along the shores of Loch Harport, offering wonderful views of the Cuillins. Production focuses on single malt Scotch whisky with special releases and distiller's editions alongside

Talisker distillery. (© Talisker)

the core range. The distillery is open all year, dependent on weather conditions.

Tours and experiences should be pre-booked. Activities on offer include immersive tasting sessions, bottling your own whisky, cask draw and tasting, a signature distillery tour, and one-off experiences such as a snapshot of Skye linking distillery cocktail tasting with an island tour undertaken by Skye Photo Academy. Special dining experiences have occasionally been provided, focusing on locally sourced food and drink. The on-site shop sells distillery produce, clothing and accessories.

TOBERMORY DISTILLERY
Tobermory
Isle of Mull
PA75 6NR
www.tobermorydistillery.com

Distilling in the area began in the 1790s with the foundation of the Ledaig distillery. It thrived until the 1930s when demand for whisky plummeted due primarily to the onset of Prohibition in America leading to the closure of the distillery. In 1993, the site was acquired by Burn Stewart Distillers, with ownership passing to Distell some twenty years later. Production under the name of the Tobermory Distillery recommenced in 2019. The distillery

▲ ***Tobermory distillery.*** (© Tobermory Distillery)

now produces an unpeated Tobermory and a peated Ledaig single malt whisky, Isle of Mull whisky, plus Tobermory gin. There are also special limited editions known as the Hebridean series, which includes spirits matured in Gonzales Byass oloroso sherry casks creating very distinct sherried whiskies, some with notes of cocoa and fruitcake.

There is a visitor centre and shop on the site, close to the A848. Visitors can book distillery tours covering the history and production of the distillery's three unique spirits, whisky and gin tasting sessions, Tobermory and Ledaig single malt whisky tastings and a warehouse experience allowing visitors to sample whisky straight from the cask. Booking in advance is recommended.

TOMATIN
Tomatin
Inverness
IV13 7YT
www.tomatin.com

Located in the village of Tomatin, outside Inverness, distilling has been taking place on the site since 1897, although the area has a whisky-making tradition dating back to the 1500s. It is extremely accessible, near Aviemore.

Owned by the Takara Shuzu company, Tomatin produces single malt and blended Scotch whisky which is

Tomatin distillery. (© Tomatin)

matured in casks. The distillery uses tall copper stills to create mellow, fruity spirits. In 2024, it launched a whisky trio of single malts single linked to three top-ranking Scottish golf courses – Royal Dornoch, St Andrews and Nairn, as a special pairing.

The visitor centre is open seven days a week. Tours of the distillery and legacy tours complete with tutored tasting sessions can be booked and it is possible to hand-fill a bottle of cask strength exclusive whisky to take home. The shop has its own bar where visitors can try a complimentary sample of the Tomatin twelve-year-old single malt.

TOLL HOUSE SPIRITS/REDCASTLE
Unit 18, Matthew Kerr Place
Arbroath
Angus
DD11 3AX
www.redcastlegin.co.uk

This is a family business producing a range of spirits and liqueurs. The premium Redcastle Spirits was launched in 2017 with a range of full strength gins, vodkas, liqueurs and rums. In 2020 a Toll House range of lower-priced spirits appeared, followed in 2023 with Broughty Ferry gin based on Angus raspberries, and a golden rum aged in oak casks.

Visitors can book Redcastle gin tasting experiences combined with an overview of how the unique flavours are created. Private gin tasting experiences can also be booked to take place at your own venue. Also available is a Redcastle blending school experience enabling visitors to make their own bespoke gin or rum. This involves exploring the background to the industry, the methods of production and identifying and choosing botanicals, before creating a personal recipe and distilling, bottling and labelling the finished product.

TORABHAIG
Teangue
Sleat
Isle of Skye
IV44 8RE
www.torabhaig.com

Torabehaig is only the second distillery ever to be licensed on the Isle of Skye. The small distillery was launched in 2017, and is located at an old farmhouse in Torabhaig which in turn was built on the site of a castle and Iron Age fort. It produces single malt Scotch whisky using traditional methods. An unusual feature of the distillery is the way in which it sets aside one month every year so that each of the nine distillers can create their own whisky from scratch. They choose every element of the distillation such as type of barley, yeast, length of fermentation, whether peaty or not, and cask type. When the whisky is ready to be bottled it becomes known as their 'journeyman cask' and bears their name.

Torabhaig distillery. (© Torbhaig)

Guided tours including a whisky and chocolate pairing activity are available and there is also a shop and café on site. Advance booking is recommended. Tours are available all year round, but the distillery is closed at weekends during the winter months.

TOULVADDIE
Fearn Aerodrome
Fearn
Inverness
IV20 1XW
www.toulvaddiedistillery.com

Toulvaddie is a micro-whisky distillery based at Fearn, in the Northern Highlands. It is located on a former Second World War RAF aerodrome and Royal Naval airbase, HMS Owl. Amazingly, the owners managed to construct the building and the flooring themselves. There is a shop and bar on site.

TULLIBARDINE
Stirling Street
Blackford
Auchterarder
Perthshire
PH4 1QG
www.tullibardine.com

The distillery began producing hand-crafted Highland single malt whisky in

Tullibardine distillery. (© Tullibardine)

the late 1940s. William Delme-Evans discovered that the purity and mineral quality of the springs in the Ochil Hills was perfect for distillation. The new distillery was named Tullibardine after the small medieval chapel nearby, making it the first distillery to be built in Scotland since 1900. Production ceased in 1993 but began again in 2003, when a group of private investors reinvigorated production. In 2011, ownership changed to the independent, French family-owned spirits company, Terroirs Distillers. Apart from malting, all production processes take place on site. The distillery has its own cooperage, maturation warehouses, blending and bottling facility. Up to 20,000 casks can be held on site for maturation. Apart from its core single malts, the distillery produces a signature range and limited editions. It also has a rare 1952 expression finished in sherry casks and possessing enhanced maltiness. Tullibardine 1952 has been described as one of the most expensive single malts worldwide. Other special custodian vintages are available such as the 1962 with aromas of flower meadows, hints of expresso, spicy nutmeg and milk chocolate coated oranges.

Guided tours are available from the visitor centre. Among the tours that can be booked are visits to the bonded warehouse or a whisky and chocolate pairing. Driver's drams are available to be taken home. Booking in advance is recommended. Tours are provided seven days a week excluding Christmas holidays.

UILE-BHEIST
Ness Bank
Inverness
IV2 4SG
www.uilebheist.com

Uile-bheist is a combination of craft brewery and distillery, set on the bank of Loch Ness. According to legend, it was at this site that the first recorded sighting of the Loch Ness Monster was noted in AD 565. Saint Columba reportedly banished a 'water monster' back into the water after it attacked one of his disciples. As a result, Uile-bheist aims to be an artisan distillery protecting the landscape as well as its legends and myths. This other-worldly ambience is reflected on the packaging and bottles. Production seeks to be sustainable and environmentally friendly.

Independently owned by founders who now run the business, the distillery was the first to be built in Inverness for 130 years and utilises innovative

▾ ***Uile-Bheist distillery.*** (© Uile-Bheist)

production methods, using some of the most advanced stills in Scotland. It produces single malt whisky from local barley and water from the River Ness, fermented with Uile-bheist's own brewers' yeast, giving it a unique character. The spirit is matured in ex-bourbon and ex-sherry casks.

The brewery uses 100% locally grown and malted barley, together with Scottish oats and water sourced from the River Ness. It produces a range of five types of beer: Inverness lager, Forest Dweller pale ale, Highland Storm Inverness session ale, White Witch unfiltered IPA and Dark Horse Highland oatmeal stout.

Uile-bheist offers a range of tours and experiences including general discovery events, whisky and beer flights and tasting sessions. There is a tap room on site offering a selection of over 200 whiskies plus craft beers. Riverbank beer gardens offer a pleasant option especially during the summer.

A waterside restaurant is located within the grounds of the Glen Mhor Hotel, offering diners a selection of sustainable local produce. The Glen Mhor hotel is located on the banks of the River Ness and combines Victorian elegance with modern comfort. Accommodation available on site ranges from hotel bedrooms to the four-bedroomed River Ness Villa. There are gin tasting sessions and a distillery tour.

WOLFBURN
Henderson Park
Thurso
Caithness
KW14 7XW
www.wolfburn.com

The Wolfburn distillery was established in 1821, and quickly became the largest distillery in Caithness. According to tax records its annual production was around 125,000 litres of proof spirit in 1826. Production continued until the 1850s. By 1872, the building lay in ruins. The remains of that original distillery can still be seen, with the new distillery a short walk away along the burn.

Planning permission was granted for a new Wolfburn distillery in 2011, and production started in 2013. A peated whisky was laid down in 2014, with the first bottle of Northland being released in 2016. During a visit by the then Prince of Wales in 2019, he apparently applied for a position at the distillery! The distillery's iconic logo derives from a drawing by Conrad Gessner, the sixteenth-century author of *The History of Four Footed Beasts and Serpents*. The image was brought to life by Scottish wildlife sculptor Carn Standing to create a seawolf sculpture that now stands on guard at the entrance.

Whisky is distilled, matured in oak, ex-bourbon or ex-oloroso sherry casks, and bottled on site. The distillery

▲ ***Seawolf standing guard at the entrance to the Wolfburn distillery.*** (© Wolfburn)

▼ ***The giant stills at Wolfburn.*** (© Wolfburn)

▲ ***Filling the casks at Wolfburn.*** (© Wolfburn)

offers a range of single malt Scotch whiskies such as Northland and Aurora, which are non-chill filtered and double distilled giving a smooth, delicate flavour. There is also the Kylver Series based on odd casks that provide a distinctive whisky. Named after a burial stone featuring the Viking runic alphabet, Wolfburn expects the Kylver Series to continue to grow in the coming years.

Distillery tours are available during weekdays at regular intervals. Each tour finishes with an opportunity to sample the various malts. Bottles and Wolfburn merchandise can be purchased on site. Advance booking is recommended.

ISLAY

ARDBEG
Port Ellen
Islay
PA42 7EA
www.ardbeg.com

John Macdougall founded Ardbeg distillery in 1815. The family continued to be actively involved in the business, even though it was sold in 1838 to a Glasgow spirits merchant, Thomas Buchanan. Interestingly, by 1853, Margaret and Flora Macdougall, Scotland's first female distillers, were running the business. It was clearly profitable as by 1887 output had risen to over 1.1 million litres a year and soon the distinctive letter A seen on its labels, together with the Ardbeg name, was trademarked. During the first half of the twentieth century, production declined and by 1981 the distillery had closed.

Blenders demanded Ardbeg whisky and this led to a resumption of small-scale distilling six years later under the ownership of Allied Lyons. Despite this demand, the distillery closed again in 1991 only to reopen in 1997 when the Glenmorangie company acquired it. Within twelve months, the business had undergone a complete change, being voted Distillery of the Year while its visitor centre and café attracted 3,500 visitors. Full production resumed in 1999, with new exclusive bottling and single casks released. In 2002, the Ardbeg Committee was formed to ensure that the distillery would 'never close again', while in 2008 Ardbeg Ten Years Old was named World Whisky of the Year. Since then there have been many new special and limited edition releases such as the Ardbeg Still Young. In 2022, the oldest ever cask released by Ardbeg, described as 'one-of-a-kind, sold for £16 million, resulting in £1 million being donated to community projects.

There is a visitor centre on site. During weekdays, visitors can book a tour and/or a sampling session. Visitors can also choose one of the tasting flights and enjoy them at leisure – no booking is required for these. There is a shop and restaurant.

An annual Ardbeg Day gathering is held at locations worldwide, including the Ardbeg distillery itself. It provides the opportunity for the launch of experimental versions, limited-time tastings and a party.

Other distilleries in Port Ellen: Laphroaig, Lagavulin, Port Ellen

ARDNAHOE

Port Askaig
Isle of Islay
PA46 7RN
www.ardnahoedistillery.com

Ardnahoe has been described as the 'long-held dream of one Scottish family'. The distillery was founded in 2015 and is wholly family-owned.

The Laing family have been involved in distilling since the 1960s when Stewart Laing began working at the Bruichladdich distillery.

It is located beside Loch Ardnahoe on the northeast of the island. The name is Scottish Gaelic for 'height of the hollow'. Distillation began in 2018. Water for use in the distillery is drawn from the loch. According to local legend, the ghost of a charging white steed rises out of the water whenever there is a full moon.

Ardnahoe distils traditional single malt whisky, possessing a combination of peaty, spicy, smoky and sweet flavours. The distillery undertakes all the production elements including malting and drying over peat smoke. Ardnahoe is one of the few Scottish distilleries still utilising traditional worm tub condensers resulting in a very slow distillation. Former bourbon and oloroso sherry casks are used to mature the resultant spirits.

There is a visitor centre and shop on site. Tours of the distillery are available between Tuesday and Saturday each week. Visitors can also enjoy tasting sessions. The Illicit Still café provides an opportunity to relax with a meal made from local produce.

Other distilleries in Port Askaig: Bunnahabhain, Caol Ila

BOWMORE
School Street
Bowmore
Isle of Islay
PA43 7JS
www.bowmore.com

Whisky distilling was first recorded on Islay in 1779. Bowmore later became the first licensed Islay distillery and is beautifully located on the shores of the Lochindaal sea loch opening out to the Atlantic Ocean. The distillery has changed hands several times throughout its history, with the most recent owners being Beam Suntory, from 2014. The distillery uses only traditional hand-crafted methods to produce single malt whisky.

The gift shop and distillery are open Tuesday to Saturday, and to pre-booked experiences on Mondays. Advance booking is recommended throughout the week. Experiences on offer include warehouse tastings, distillery tours and a vaults secrets tour.

An annual gathering of whisky and Islay fans takes place during the last week of May. It celebrates the whisky, the island and the culture.

The distillery has accommodation available for visitors at the Bowmore Cottages. Constructed in a traditional Islay cottage style, they were built in the 1800s and provided a home to distillery workers. All the cottages have been fully restored and renovated and can be booked for a minimum of three nights. They are located close to the shoreline.

BRUICHLADDICH
Isle of Islay
PA49 7UN
www.uk.bruichladdich.com

Bruichladdich began producing whisky in 1881 but was closed in 1994. It was resurrected in 2001 by a consortium of whisky enthusiasts using the old buildings and warehouses. All the bottling is undertaken on site. The company aims to be a pioneer, reconnecting a sustainable environment and the resultant produce. The unpeated single malt whisky is produced using a slow fermentation through tall, narrow stills using Islay spring water. In 2012, the ownership changed when Rémy Cointreau purchased it.

It produces three single malt Scotch whiskies (Bruichladdich, Port Charlotte and Octomore) using only traditional methods, with bottling taking place on site. The distillery also produces The Botanist gin.

Pre-booked tours of the Victorian distillery are available, exploring how the single malt whisky and The Botanist gin are produced. There are guided tours introducing the history and methods used on site, tasting sessions and a warehouse experience. The distillery shop is open for tastings and general retail during trading hours. Between April and October, Bruichladdich is open seven days a week, while over the winter period it opens Monday to Saturday.

Other distilleries in Bruichladdich: Kilchoman

BUNNAHABHAIN
Port Askaig
Isle of Islay
PA46 7AP
www.bunnahabhain.com

Located on the edge of Bunnahabhain Bay along the shores of the Sound of Islay, the name is derived from the Gaelic word meaning 'mouth of the river'. A remote location, there is just a single track road leading to the distillery. Founded in 1881, distillation has taken place almost continuously ever since. Until the 1960s when a road was built, all the whisky was distributed and supplies received by sea. Additional stills were added in 1963 due to the scale of demand for Bunnahabain whisky. Bunnahabain was purchased by Burn Stewart Distillers in 2003, and was subsequently totally rebranded and the packaging redesigned. In 2010, Bunnahabhain started to produce non-chill filtered and natural-coloured beverages.

Bunnhabhain produces unpeated Islay single malt whisky using pure spring water from the River Margadale. Maturation is undertaken in ex-sherry casks. The range includes distillery exclusives and limited editions.

A visitor centre was opened 2021. The distillery is open seven days a week, with pre-booking required for tours and tasting experiences.

Other distilleries in Port Askaig: Ardnahoe, Caol ila

CAOL ILA
Port Askaig
Isle of Islay
PA46 7RL
www.malts.com/en-row/brands/caol-ila

Founded in 1846 by Hector Henderson, the Caol Ila Distillery is now owned by

Caol Ila distillery. (© Caol Ila/Diageo)

Diageo. The name is pronounced 'cull eela'. It is beautifully located on the rugged east coast of Islay facing the stunning Paps of Jura. Caol Ila is the home of Johnnie Walker whisky. The site also produces a range of specialist Caol Ila single malts. All the barley is malted locally at Port Ellen. Water supplies come from springs rising in the nearby Loch Nam Burn.

Distillery tours can be booked and include an immersive experience followed by a guided tasting session. Other tours include a flavour journey and a sleeping still session during the 'silent season'. There is also an on site bar and retail area available to visitors.

Other distilleries in Port Askaig: Ardnahoe, Bunnahbhain

ISLE OF ISLAY GIN
Islay Gin Ltd
Visitor Centre
Islay Square
Bridgend
Isle of Islay
PA44 7NZ
www.isleofislaygin.co.uk

A small independent family distillery, founded in 2017 which creates a range of four premium gins including Nerabus Gorse gin and Nerabus Heather gin. There are no distillery tours available, but there is a visitor centre located in the grounds of Islay House providing information about the distillery. It acts as a shop and tasting area. A wide variety of local products are also sold. The visitor centre is open Tuesday to Saturday only.

KILCHOMAN
Rockside Farm
Bruichladdich
Isle of Islay
PA49 7UT
www.kilchomandistillery.com

This artisan farm distillery has led the way in reviving traditional farm distilling. Every element involved in the production, from growing the barley to bottling, takes place on the farm. Founded in 2005, it was the first to be built on the island for over 120 years. A family-run business, the aim has always been to follow a 100% Islay production philosophy. The Single Farm single malt whisky is matured in former sherry or bourbon casks. It is non-chill filtered and natural coloured. Kilchoman produces a wide range of artisan whisky catering for varying tastes including rich and fruity, spicy chocolate and rich peat, citrus layered with vanilla and butterscotch. There are also special limited editions.

The visitor centre was opened in 2020 as a base for informal and comprehensive tastings, as well as guided tours of the distillery. The Kilchoman shop stocks all the whisky ranges including distillery-exclusive casks that can only be purchased by visitors to the site. The café offers a range of home-made produce and barista-style coffees.

Other distilleries in Bruichladdich: Bruichladdich

Kilchoman distillery. (© **Kilchoman**)

LAGAVULIN
Lagavulin
Port Ellen
Isle of Islay
Argyll
PA42 7DZ
www.malts.com/en-row/distilleries/lagavulin

One of the oldest distilleries on the Isle of Islay, Lagavulin whisky has been made here for over 200 years. The first legal whisky was produced in 1816. Ownership of the distillery has changed hands several times over the years, and is now owned by Diageo. Located on the edge of Lagavulin Bay on the southern side of the island, it produces smoky, peaty single malt whiskies from unusual pear shaped stills. The Lagavulin brand has been referred to in various films such as being the preferred drink of DC Comics supervillain Lex Luther.

A range of tours and experiences are available and include sensory tasting sessions, a classic tour and a warehouse experience. Booking tours and experiences in advance is recommended. In addition to core ranges, several exclusive whiskies are only available from the distillery itself, such as the Lagavulin Jazz Exclusive.

Other distilleries in Port Ellen: Ardbeg, Laphroaig, Port Ellen

Lagavulin distillery. (© Lagavulin)

LAPHROAIG
Port Ellen
Isle of Islay
Argyll
PA42 7DU
www.laphroaig.com

Sited on Loch Laphroaig on the southern side of the Islay, Laphroaig distillery was founded in 1825 by brothers Donald and Alexander Johnston using water from the soft peaty Kilbride stream. Ownership changed several times over the next 150 years. It is now owned by Beam Suntory, the American subsidiary of Japan's Suntory Holdings. When King Charles III was Prince of Wales he granted Laphroaig a Royal Warrant, which he awarded in person during a visit to the distillery. Laphroaig produces single malt whisky, and claims to be the 'most richly flavoured of all Scotch whiskies'. The majority of its whisky is aged to ten years, with older versions being rare and expensive. Some expressions are aged in white port and Madeira casks while others use sherry oak or bourbon.

Tours and tasting sessions are available. These include experience tours, wood exploration experiences, 'Laphroaig Past and Present', 'Heart of Laphroaig', behind the scenes tours and an unusual guided walk through the local countryside with its links to the production of whisky. Pre-booking is essential. Laphroaig Day is held once a year as part of the Islay Whisky Festival involving music, dance and sporting events. During Laphroaig Day, visitors have access to talks, tours and tasting drams straight from the barrel.

Other distilleries in Port Ellen: Ardbeg, Lagavulin, Port Ellen

PORT ELLEN
Kiln Square
Port Ellen
Isle of Islay
PA42 7AF
www.malts.com/en-row/brands/port-ellen

Originally founded in 1825, For over four decades Port Ellen distillery was one of the countless 'ghost distilleries' mothballed by its owners. In 2024, owners Diageo reopened the site and resumed whisky production. Work has been undertaken to decarbonise the site and increase distillery capacity.

Visitors are welcome to take part in immersive tours and tastings designed to explore the distillery history and its future. One of the more unusual experiences is 'Atlas of Smoke', which investigates the mysterious flavours and dimensions of smoke, with its effects on whisky. All tours and experiences have to be pre-booked. There is no walk-in facility.

Other distilleries in Port Ellen: Ardbeg, Lagavulin, Laphroaig

LOWLAND

56 NORTH
2 West Crosscauseway
Newington
Edinburgh
EH8 9JP
www.fiftysixnorth.co.uk

Reputed to be the Scotland's original gin bar, 56 North comes complete with a working distillery trading as the South Loch Distillery. Over 300 gins and spirits are stocked here, and food is served daily. South Loch began distilling gin on the site in 2017 and uses 50-litre copper pot stills. Ranges include various fruity flavours such as Spiced Cranberry & Clementine, Citrus and Lime Flower and Black Raspberry Old Tom gin.

There is a range of experiences available that can be booked including an introduction to the South Loch distillery and a tasting session, Scottish gin and cheese pairings and a traditional Scottish haggis paired with various tastings of whiskies and gins.

Other distilleries in Edinburgh: Eden Mill, Edinburgh Gin, Holyrood, Johnnie Walker, Lind & Lime, One Poison, One Square, Port of Leith, Summerhall/ Pickering's gin, The Scotch Whisky Experience

1881 DISTILLERY & GIN SCHOOL
Peebles Hydro
Innerleithen Road
Peebles
Peebleshire
EH45 8LX
www.1881distillery.com

Possessing its own private spring known as the Shieldgreen, Peebles Hydro dates back to 1881. It provided hydrotherapy and a hotel with a guaranteed clean water supply for affluent visitors wanting to escape city pollution. The purity of the waters at the Peebles Hydro became legendary for helping numerous ailments. The hotel is now part of the Crieff Family of hotels, offering

▸ ***Making gin at 1881 distillery.*** (© 1881)

▲ ***Peebles Hydro 1881 distillery gin school.***
(© Peebles Hydro 1881 distillery)

accommodation all year round together with a range of activities such as alpaca trekking, archery, axe throwing and mountain biking, as well as a gin school.

The Shieldgreen spring also provides water for the onsite 1881 gin distillery. Visitors can enjoy a gin and tonic which uses all local ingredients – the gin with locally sourced botanicals as well as the tonic water itself. Four premium gins are produced on site: London Dry, Pavilion Pink, Subtly Smoked and Navy Strength.

Visitors can book a tour of the distillery, which includes learning about the history of the Peebles Hydro, and see the stills.

The gin school is the largest residential gin school in the UK and is actually located in what was once the hydro swimming pool. There are twenty-six individual copper stills which can be used by participants on the gin school courses to make their own bespoke gin.

ANNANDALE
Northfield
Annan
Dumfrieshire
DG12 5LL
www.annandaledistillery.com

Established in 1836, Annandale is one of Scotland's oldest distilleries and was once owned by Johnnie Walker & Sons. The distillery closed in 1918, and was eventually reborn in 2007 when major restoration began, enabling the historic buildings to be reused. Production restarted in 2014 with the first whisky cases being left to mature in the original warehouse dating from the 1830s. Annandale's single malt whisky is available in both peated and unpeated styles. It's Man O'Words and Man O'Sword whiskies are named after Robert Burns and Robert the Bruce.

A visitor centre was opened by the Princess Royal in 2015 and now welcomes over 25,000 people every year. Annandale has an on-site café and offers hourly tours of the distillery. Wedding and corporate packages are available, along with cask ownership and whisky by the dram, bottle or barrel. The on-site shop sells a range of whisky, plus merchandise and gift vouchers. All tours must be pre-booked.

Other distilleries in Dumfrieshire: Bladnoch, Crafty, Dark Art, Moffat

AUCHTENTOSHAN
Great Western Road
Dalmuir
Clydebank
Glasgow
G81 4SJ
www.auchentoshan.com

Now owned by Beam Suntory, the distillery was set up by an engineer from Greenock in 1823. Ownership changed several times over the years, and in 1941 whisky production stopped due to German bombing of the River Clyde and its shipyards. Production resumed in the late 1940s. Auchtentoshan whisky is triple distilled, and left to mature in bourbon, sherry or fine wine casks for at least three years. There is a core range, aged range and special editions such as three wood single malt whiskies matured in three different types of wooden casks, dark oak and blood oak single malt whiskies.

The visitor centre is open seven days a week. It includes a shop selling Auchtentoshan whisky and related merchandise. A selection of tours can be booked exploring how Auchtentoshan makes whisky, including the 'Essence' tour and detailed whisky tasting sessions in the tasting lounge.

Other distilleries in the Glasgow area: Clydesdale, Crossbill, Glengoyne, Jackton

BIGGAR GIN COMPANY
The Stillhouse
Wyndales Mill
Symington
Biggar
South Lanarkshire
ML12 6HX
www.biggargin.com

A family business, Biggar focuses on small-batch spirits of around 140 bottles at a time. These are primarily premium rum, vodka and gin. Its original recipe for gin includes botanicals like rowan berries and nettles. The most recent products are an Old Tom gin and a herbaceous recipe gin. Clyde Valley plum gin is a seasonal offering infused with plums from the local area. The company has also launched an Asian spiced rum using Biggar's own blend of Scottish white rum with a white Caribbean rum.

Distilling began in 2019, using a purpose-built stillhouse and traditional copper pot stills. Tours of the distillery operate every Tuesday and Friday, and include sampling core spirits and an experimental recipe. Occasional longer distillery tours focusing on mixology can be arranged. All tours must be pre-booked.

Other distilleries in Lanarkshire: Wee Farm

BLACKNESS BAY
Shore Road
Blackness on Sea
Linlithgow
Lothian
EH49 7NL
www.blacknessbaydistillery.co.uk

An independent distillery producing whisky and rum, Blackness Bay distillery is located on the Firth of Forth and occupies the oldest building in the village. The views from the distillery are quite spectacular. Only traditional production methods are used, together with locally sourced barley.

The spirits are pot stilled in twin copper vessels before being matured in oak barrels. The blended whisky uses whiskies from both the Lowlands and the Highlands so as to capture the nature of Blackness Bay. Also produced on site is a new-make spirit taking less time to mature. According to Blackness it is characterised by a 'magical earthiness and a rich depth of flavour' reminiscent of Irish poteen.

The distillery has its own adjoining pub/restaurant, The Lobster Pot. Tasting sessions and tours are available, especially for small groups.

▲***Blackness Bay distillery.*** (© Blackness Bay)

▼***Blackness Bay distillery production area.*** (Blackness Bay)

The tour shows how Blackness turns local grain from nearby Alloa into whisky, describes the history of distilling in the area and provides snippets of local history. This is an area that has a fascinating heritage, linked with Mary Queen of Scots, the Jacobites, a castle besieged by Cromwell and the poet Robert Burns. Pre-booking is essential.

Other distilleries in Lothian: Glenkinchie, Linlithgow, NB Distillery, Secret Garden

BLADNOCH
Bladnoch
Newton Stewart
Dumfries & Galloway
DG8 9AB
www.uk.bladnoch.com

Bladnoch is one of the oldest and largest privately-owned Scottish distillers, founded in 1817 when John and Thomas McClelland were given a licence to distil whisky on their farm. It stayed in family hands for almost a century and became extremely successful, gaining the title of 'Queen of the Lowlands'. During the twentieth century, ownership changed several times. In 2015, Australian entrepreneur David Prior acquired the distillery and two years of renovation began. Bladnoch produces a range of peaty single malt Scotch whiskies covering signature, aged and limited editions, which are matured in a variety of former sherry, oak, bourbon and California red wine casks.

In 2019, visitor centre activities were revamped to include new experiences, a gift shop selling Bladnoch whisky and a café. A range of tours and tasting sessions can be booked including the 'Classic' tour and an opportunity use the tools and equipment to analyse malted barley, wash and spirit. The centre is open Tuesday to Saturday. Distillery tours are by appointment only.

Other distilleries in Dumfries & Galloway: Annadale, Crafty, Dark Art, Moffat

BORDERS
Commercial Road
Hawick
Roxburghshire
TD9 7AQ
www.thebordersdistillery.com

Located in a riverside building which was once an Edwardian electrical works, Borders is the first Scotch whisky distillery in the area since 1837. Borders distillery sources all its barley from local farmers within a thirty-five mile radius. All the 'Made in Hawick' products are completely distilled at the distillery in oak casks. The range available includes blended whisky using various Scottish single malts, new-make spirit, malt and rye whisky,

▲ ***The rare Carterhead still at Borders distillery.*** (© Borders)

malted barley vodka and Kerr's gin. The Workshop new-make series highlights experimental liquids forming stepping stones in the creation of the first Borders single malt.

An unusual feature of the distillery is the rare Carter-Head still, used to create the Puffing Billy Steam vodka. Rather than using standard filtration methods, the spirit is steamed through charcoal in the still and never filtered as a liquid. The resulting malted barley vodka is the only vodka worldwide created as a result of this method of

▲ ***Inside Borders distillery.*** (© Borders)

distilling, which gives a very creamy beverage. The same Carter-Head still is used to produce Kerr's gin, enabling botanicals to be steamed in the spirit vapours.

Guided tours of the distillery are given by one of the company's distillers, and show the distillery in full use. The building incorporates many unique features relating to its former use, and recycles many of the old structures and furnishings. It is a comprehensive tour covering all the various spirits and ends with a sampling session in the distillery bar. Tours must be pre-booked and are available between the end of March and the end of October. The visitor centre is open Monday to Saturday all year round.

Other distilleries in Roxburghshire: Lillard

CLYDESIDE
100 Stobcross Road
Glasgow G3 8QQ
www.theclydeside.com

Owned by the Morrison family, Clydeside is located on the former Queen Dock. Their ancestors helped build the original docklands over a century ago, and possess a long history

▲ ***Clydeside distillery.*** (© Clydeside)

with other well known distilleries in the area such as Glen Garioch and Bowmore. The distillery is based in the Pumphouse, a historic building once used by Customs and Excise to keep an eye on whisky exports.

Clydeside distils single malt whisky on the site using water derived from Loch Katrine in the West Highlands, and barley from Scottish Lowland farms. Whisky is matured in bourbon and sherry casks, resulting in a delicate Lowland style.

Visitor facilities are available on site including a café and distillery shop selling single malt whisky from all over Scotland, bespoke bottles and premium selections. The distillery is open seven days a week. Tours and whisky tasting experiences can be pre-booked. Along with the 'Clydeside Experience' tour, you can also book a tour with a chocolate and whisky tasting or an exclusive behind-the-scenes tour with the distillery manager.

Other distilleries in the Glasgow area: Auchtenoshan, Crossbill, Glengoyne, Jackton

▲ ***Clydeside distillery: tour of the stillhouse.*** (© Clydeside)

CRAFTY
Wigtown Road
Newton Stewart
Dumfries & Galloway
DG8 6AS
www.craftydistillery.com

Founded in 2017 by Graham Taylor, this independent distillery has been described as one of Scotland's 'most innovative distilleries', pioneering new methods resulting in a smooth, new-make spirit. It also produces a range of gins. The hillside location is spectacular, offering views towards the Galloway Hills.

The site includes a shop and the Tree Bar, made from a 3 tonne piece of local Douglas fir. Visitors can take part in a behind-the-scenes tour, exploring how Crafty's single malt Scotch whisky is produced and ending with a sampling session. Tours must be booked in advance.

Special events are held at Crafty throughout the year include cocktail sessions and pop-up food venues.

Other distilleries in Dumfries & Galloway: Annadale, Bladnoch, Dark Art, Moffat

▲ ***Crafty distillery.*** (© Crafty)

▼ ***The tasting room at Crafty.*** (© Crafty)

CROSSBILL
Unit 1
Barras Art & Design
54 Calton Entry
Glasgow
G40 2SB
www.crossbilgin.com

Originally set up in 2012 in Aviemore, Crossbill moved to Glasgow in 2017. The company creates a range of hand-crafted gins, which it states are 'a celebration of Scottish nature, made with wild, fresh botanicals, harvested by hand then slowly macerated in Glasgow before being distilled'. Typical gins include Crossbill Red dry and the Crossbill Green dry. The brand is named after the rare Scottish crossbill, a small finch which nests in conifers alongside the juniper bushes.

Crossbill has its own gin school where visitors can create their own bespoke gin. There are various options available including tasting sessions, gin and chocolate pairing, classes on distilling and a blending class, involving learning how to combine pre-distilled botanical spirits to create a gin. All sessions must be pre-booked.

Other distilleries in Glasgow area: Auchtenoshan, Clydesdale, Glengoyne, Jackton

DARK ART
The Johnson
St Mary Street
Kirkcudbright
Dumfries & Galloway
DG6 4EG
www.darkartdistillery.com

Dark Art distillery. (© Dark Art)

Dark Art is a craft distillery opened in 2021 by Andrew Clark Hutchinson, whose family have lived in Kirkcudbright for generations. It claims to be Scotland's most southerly distillery. Originally built decades ago as a primary school, reminders of that use can be seen everywhere, including old-style chalkboards, wood panelling and the central tower clock.

Dark Art produces a range of dry gins inspired by the local area, especially the dark skies for which Galloway is known. This is one of the darkest places in Europe, and is an accredited Dark Sky Park, making it the perfect place to explore the sky and stars at night. The Northern Lights are sometimes visible here. Dark Art's first gin was the aptly named Sky Garden, followed by the UnderStory gin, inspired by the dark corners created by the trees in the Galloway Forest. Dark Art has also introduced Scotland's first 100% agave spirit, known as Véspero Blanco.

The distillery includes a visitor centre and shop providing gin tours and tastings. Distillery tours must be pre-booked. Sharing the site with Dark Art are several other tenants such as a pottery painting studio and a dark space planetarium.

Other distilleries in Dumfries & Galloway: Annadale, Bladnoch, Craft, Moffat

▲ ***Sky Garden gin.*** (© Dark Sky)

▲ ***UnderStory gin.*** (© Dark Sky)

▲ ***Véspero Blanco, Scotland's first agave spirit.*** (© Dark Art)

▼ ***Darnley's at Kingsbarns.*** (© Darnleys/Kingsbarns)

DARNLEY'S GIN
Darnley's Gin Cottage
East Newhall Farm
Kingsbarns
Fife
KY16 8QE
www.darnleysgin.com

A family business, Darnley's also operates the nearby Kingsbarns whisky distillery. Many of the botanicals used in the creation of its gins are grown in the garden surrounding the cottage, or are foraged locally. The London dry style gin is made in a copper pot still located in the cottage. No additional additives or sugars are added after distillation. Darnley produces a range of gins including Original gin, Spiced gin, Navy strength and limited blends such as Smoke and Zest.

Visitors can pre-book a guided tasting, tour and talk, discovering the history of Darnley's gin, the background to gin production and the botanicals involved in the creation of the gin. There is also a 'Ginspiration' tour involving a guided tour of the distillery, a tasting session plus the creation of a bespoke gin and tonic. The day-long gin school offers the opportunity to create a bespoke gin on an individual or shared basis.

Other distilleries in Fife: Eden Mill, Inchdairnie, Kingsbarns, Lindores, Tayport

EDEN MILL
Guardbridge
St Andrews
KY16 9PB
1A Rutland Place
Edinburgh
EH1 2AD
www.edenmill.com

Eden Mill is a new purpose-built distillery opened in 2024 on the coast of St Andrews, overlooking the estuary. By opening a whisky and gin distillery at this site, Eden Mill is reviving an industry that has been practised here

Eden Mill distillery, St Andrews. (© Eden Mill)

for centuries. During the mid 1800s, it was the site of the Seggie whisky distillery. The new distillery is designed to be as sustainable as possible, using only 100% renewable electricity and all CO_2 produced during the fermentation process is captured for use by the adjacent university campus.

Eden Mill offers a wide range of premium gins, gin liqueurs and single malt whiskies. The first whisky bottling took place in 2018, and Eden Mill whisky has a gentle character with notes of citrus, honey and spices.

Open to visitors all year round, it offers distillery tours, sampling sessions, bar and café. The café is on the ground floor, while the bar is located on the top floor of the distillery building, offering spectacular coastal views.

In Edinburgh, visitors can take part in various experiences at its Rutland Place location. These include a whisky masterclass, the 'Gin Story' and cocktail-making.

All tours and experiences at both sites need to be pre-booked.

Other distilleries in Fife: Darnley's Gin, Inchdairnie, Kingsbarns, Lindores, Tayport

Other distilleries in Edinburgh: 56 North, Edinburgh gin, Holyrood, Johnnie Walker, Lind & Lime, Old Poison, One Square, Port of Leith, Summerhall/ Pickering's gin, The Scotch Whisky Experience

EDINBURGH GIN AT THE ARCHES
East Market Street
Old Town
Edinburgh
www.edinburghgin.com

Formed in 2010 by two entrepreneurs, Alex and Jane Nichol, the distillery was sold in 2016 to Ian MacLeod Distilleries.

Edinburgh Gin produces a wide range of London dry gins, flavoured gins, gin liqueurs and pre-mixed cans. The distillery is known for its flavour innovations such as Cranachan gin (inspired by the classic Scottish desert) and Tiramisu gin. A distillery exclusive is sold only at the distillery itself.

Originally the distillery operated from a site in the west of Edinburgh, moving to a new site at The Arches in the Old Town in 2024. The Arches site is set against a backdrop of the historic Trinity Church. Historically, this is a very significant site since it was home to the one of the original physic gardens, which later moved to become part of the Royal Botanical Gardens. The distillation process involves three new stills and uses only 100% natural flavours.

The Arches includes a visitor centre offering guided tours exploring the intriguing history of gin-making in Edinburgh as well as a range of immersive tasting sessions. These include a gin-making experience in the distillery's exclusive gin laboratory.

▲ **Edinburgh gin distillery at the Arches in the Old Town.** (© Edinburgh Gin)

Other distilleries in Edinburgh: 56 North, Eden Mill, Holyrood, Johnnie Walker, Lind & Lime, Old Poison, One Square, Port of Leith, Summerhall/Pickering's gin, The Scotch Whisky Experience

FALKIRK
Grandsable Road
Polmont
Falkirk
Stirlingshire
FK2 0WA
www.falkirkdistillery.com

A family business, Falkirk distillery began by building its own Lowland whisky distillery over a decade ago amidst the historic surroundings of a UNESCO World Heritage Site. The distillery sourced its own artesian well on the site, and created buildings and processes designed to reflect the key ethos of 'place, people, family and the future'. Inaugural whisky releases came from first-run new-make spirit laid down in 2020. The whisky is free from artificial colouring and non-chill filtered.

▲ ***Falkirk's 4.6 tonne mash tun.*** (© Falkirk)

Tours of the distillery are available by appointment only and must be pre-booked. A tasting session is included in the tour.

Other distilleries in Stirlingshire: Rosebank, Stirling

GLENGOYNE
Dumgoyne
Near Killearn
Glasgow
G63 9LB
www.glengoyne.com

Visit Scotland describes Glengoyne as the country's most beautiful distillery, situated in a hidden glen next to a waterfall. It is located close to Loch Lomond. It aims to be as sustainable and environmentally friendly as possible, using local sourcing, recyclable packaging, renewable electricity and honey from its own beehives. The company distils single malt whisky. Since 2003, Ian Macleod Distillers Ltd, an independent family business, has owned Glengoyne.

▲ ***Glengoyne distillery.*** (© Glengoyne)

The isolated site led distilling to begin secretly in 1820, before acquiring a licence in 1833 trading as Glenguin of Burnfoot. Local fuel was used in the distillation rather than peat and the whisky was matured in sherry barrels. The storms of 1888 led to reports of casks from Glenguin's Glasgow warehouses being washed down the river – with only broken and empty casks being eventually returned. Ten years later, the distillery manager drowned in the distillery loch and it is said that his ghost still haunts the grounds. In 1907, the company changed its name to Glengoyne. In 1970 the distillery's name attracted attention when a large container fell off a lorry in Glasgow. According to media reports of the period, businessmen and housewives walked away licking their fingers, while bottles, cups, tumblers and teapots appeared out of nowhere. Late in 2020, Glengoyne launched a fifty-year-old Highland single malt.

Access is possible seven days a week. Visitors can enjoy a range of distillery tours, tastings and experiences such as an opportunity to create your own single malt in the sample room. Booking in advance is recommended. There is a shop on site.

Other distilleries in the Glasgow area: Auchtenoshan, Clydesdale, Crossbill, Jackton

GLENKINCHIE
Pencaitland
Tranent
East Lothian
EH34 5ET
www.malts.com/en-gb/distilleries/glenkinchie

Located just fifteen miles from Edinburgh, Glenkinchie is one of the 'Four Corners' distilleries of Johnny Walker. Glenkinchie distils one of the key ingredients – Edinburgh malt. The visitor centre offers an opportunity to see introductory and archival exhibitions relating to Johnny Walker whisky. Special events are frequently held, including masterclasses and collaborations with local suppliers.

Visitors are encouraged to explore the Victorian distillery, with its orchards and wildflower areas. A range of tours and experiences are available including warehouse tastings, 'Distillery After Dark' and 'Flavour Journey'.

Advance booking is required for tours and experiences. No tours of the distillery are provided during the 'silent season' from April to early June. There is an on-site shop.

Other distilleries in Lothian: Blackness Bay, NB, Linlithgow, Secret Garden

HOLYROOD
19 St Leonard's Lane
Edinburgh
EH8 9SH
www.holyrooddistillery.co.uk

Established in 2019, Holyrood distillery is sited in the historic centre of Edinburgh's Old Town. From the beginning it set out to be different, seeking to create a different type of whisky and exploring new ways of using heritage malts, speciality malts and yeasts in the production process to create a broader range of flavours. Holyrood aims to be among the 'finest spirit maker in the world' stressing the need to 'test, learn, improve, repeat' as its research mindset when creating its varied range of spirits.

Holyrood produces ranges of single malt whisky, single cask whisky, new make, rum, gin and strong waters. It has reintroduced historic concepts such as strong waters – a barley-based spirit that was common in the 1800s. Two types of strong waters have been created combining barley with a neutral wheat spirit resulting in a creamy Chevalier and a new-make Golden Promise, possessing aromatic notes of citrus and pepper. Other

Holyrood distillery. (© Holyrood)

Holyrood brands include the Height of Arrows gin varieties, Elizabeth Yard Savannah rum, New Make Crystal malt, New Make Chocolate malt and New Make Black Cork. Bottles from the single cask whisky range tend to be limited editions only, selling out quickly, while the single malts are more readily available and are created using a variety of specialty malts matured using bourbon barrels.

Inspiration for many of Holyrood's spirits has come from Edinburgh's history and heritage. Black Cork was a legendary eighteenth- and nineteenth-century local beer, and Holyrood reflects this beer in its new make, using a complex combination of peated and roasted malts to imitate the old coal fires of Edinburgh.

Holyrood offers visitors a range of tours and tasting experiences, all of which should be pre-booked. The 'Signature' tour explores gin and whisky production spaces, along with sample tastings throughout the tour. A shorter experience is provided by the 'Holyrood Highlights' whisky experience which involves a look at the whisky production area, and a tutored tasting of a single malt whisky. The 'Journey to Whisky' tour is ideal for whisky enthusiasts as it offers a more in-depth exploration of malt whisky production, discovering how the company sets out to push the boundaries with its experimental flavour approach.

There are daily self-guided flight tastings provided, also gin tasting experiences and a whisky tasting experience involving some of Holyrood's finest expressions. One of the more unusual visitor experiences available at Holyrood is a walking tour of the city's brewing and distilling heritage. It covers the forgotten breweries of Edinburgh's Southside, how the brewing industry has helped shape the city plus stories of the infamous 'Charmed Circle'.

Holyrood distillery is very accessible by public transport and is just fifteen minutes from the Royal Mile, beside Holyrood Park. There is an onsite distillery bar and shop.

Other distilleries and related attractions in Edinburgh: 56 North, Eden Mill, Edinburgh Gin, Johnnie Walker, Lind & Lime, Old Poison, One Square, Port of Leith, Summerhall/Pickering's Gin, The Scotch Whisky Experience

INCHDAIRNIE

Whitecraigs Road
Glenrothes
Fife
KY6 2RX
www.inchairniedistillery.com

Located on the banks of the River Leven in Fife, the distillery was founded in 2011, with distillation beginning in December 2015. The first distillate was Strathenry, a single malt exchanged with other distillers and blenders. Distillation of the first InchDairnie single malt using Fife barley began in 2016, combining seasonal whisky distillations across the year. This will be released as a vintage in 2029, creating a complex single malt. In 2017, the company began distilling rye-based peated single malt, plus a combination InchDairnie malted rye and barley known as RyeLaw. Further innovation came in 2019, when InchDairnie distilled an oak spirit, believed to the first time this has been undertaken in Scotland, while in 2022 it distilled winter barley usually only used for dark ale brewing. Such innovations reflect the adventurous nature of this distillery, which likes to explore flavour, pushing the boundaries of Scotch whisky. For example, it uses an unusual mash filter which extracts more sugar, affecting flavour, and different types of grain.

Other distilleries in Fife: Darnley's gin, Eden Mill, Kingsbarns, Lindores, Tayport

JACKTON

RAER Spirits,
Hayhill Road,
Jackton,
Glasgow
G74 5AN
www.raer.co.uk

A privately-owned business, Jackton began distilling in 2020, laying down its first cask that year. Maturation is undertaken using oak, sherry, rum, port and wine casks. It produces a new-make spirit using locally malted Scotch barley but aims to grow its own barley on the Jackton Estate. The company is currently creating its own maltings facility. Its blended RAER Scotch whisky has been described as being rich and warm, with hints of citrus and caramel. An award-winning distillery, Jackton also produces a range of gins such as Rose gin and Something Blue gin, plus a vodka.

Although the distillery is not open to the public, it does have an on-site shop where visitors are welcome to enjoy samples of the various spirits. The shop also stocks related hand-crafted merchandise such as glassware and clothing. The shop is open weekdays, with limited opening on Saturdays.

Other distilleries in Glasgow: Auchtenoshan, Clydesdale, Crossbill, Glengoyne

JOHNNIE WALKER PRINCES STREET
145 Princes Street
Edinburgh
www.johnniewalker.com/en-gb/visit-us-princes-street

Located on Edinburgh's prestigious Princes Street, this is an immersive experience designed to take visitors through the 200-year history of Johnny Walker Scotch whisky. The eight-floor building also provides food and drink facilities at its many bars and restaurants, such as the 1820 rooftop bar which has stunning views across the city towards Edinburgh Castle. There are Michelin-starred whisky and food pairings available. Visitors are also able to buy Johnnie Walker whisky and other merchandise such as limited edition bottles.

Visitors can book an immersive experiential signature tour involving live performances, light shows and whisky cocktails. The tour can even be tailored to personal tastebuds when visitors take the Johnnie Walker flavour quiz to identify personal flavour profiles. Tour participants gain a discount on all products and merchandise sold in the store on the day of the visit as well as a discount on drinks in the 1820 bar. Other potential tours available include a visit to the Whisky Maker's Cellar, tutored tastings in the Explorers' Bothy, whisky and

artisanal chocolate pairings, a Johnnie Walker Blue Label and umami tasting experience and what is described as the ultimate whisky experience: 'Johnnie Walker & Glenkinchie'.

The site is easily accessible to pedestrians and via public transport as is only ten minutes from Haymarket train station. It is open seven days a week.

Other distilleries and related attractions in the area: 56 North, Eden Mill, Edinburgh Gin, Holyrood, Lind & Lime, Old Poison, One Square, Port of Leith, Summerhall/Pickering's Gin, The Scotch Whisky Experience

KINGSBARNS
East Newhall Farm
Kingsbarns
Fife
KY16 8QE
www.kingsbarnsdistillery.com

Kingsbarns is owned by the Wemyss family, who have a long history of involvement in the whisky industry. John Haig, founder of Haig's, built his first distillery on land owned by the Wemyss family back in the early nineteenth century. The distillery is located in an old Georgian farm building on the Wemyss Estate. The first casks were filled in 2015. Kingsbarns produces a range of single malt whiskies and gins. Typical produce includes Balcomie sherry cask matured and Kingsbarns flagship Doocot.

The distillery first opened to the public in 2014, and offers an opportunity for visitors to explore the process of making whisky. Located in a rural area, the visitor centre is open daily. There is a shop and café with an outdoor seating area. Various experiences are available including a Kingsbarns 'Introductory' guided tour,

Visitors arriving at Kingsbarns distillery. (© Kingsbarns)

the 'Nineteenth Hole' tour, a gin tour, and a 'Ginspiration' tasting session. All activities should be pre-booked. The visitor centre is open seven days a week.

Other distilleries in Fife: Darnley's Gin, Eden Mill, Inchdairnie, Lindores, Tayport

LIND & LIME
24 Coburg Street
Edinburgh
EH6 6HB
www.lindandlime.com

Set up in 2017, Lind & Lime produces a London dry gin based on a balance of tastes reflecting the heritage and industry of Edinburgh, and its historic distilling district of Leith. It aims to be as sustainable as possible. The company is B Corp certified, using 100% organic ingredients, 100% green electricity and 100% plastic-free packaging.

Lind & Lime offers pre-booked tours such as a tour of the distillery, along with tasting, bottle-filling and cocktail-making. It also organises bespoke experiences, private dinners, tasting menus and other events on request.

Other distilleries and related attractions in Edinburgh: 56 North, Eden Mill, Edinburgh Gin, Holyrood, Johnnie Walker, Old Poison, One Square, Port of Leith, Summerhall/Pickering's Gin, The Scotch Whisky Experience

LILLIARD GIN
Lanton Mill
Jedburgh
Roxburghshire
TD8 6ST
www.lilliardgin.co.uk

A craft gin company, Lilliard is located in a tiny cowshed turned distillery in the pretty Teviot Valley near Jedburgh.

It is open to the public at weekends only, or by special arrangement at other times. Tours and private gin-making classes can be arranged. Also on site is a café, shop, brewery and grass-sledging activities while resident ospreys circle in the skies.

Other distilleries in the area: Borders

LINDORES ABBEY
Abbey Road
Newburgh
Fife
KY14 6HH
www.lindoresabbeydistillery.com

The McKenzie Smith family acquired the site over 100 years ago. In 2017, the family-run distillery was opened on farmland directly opposite the ruins with the aim of restoring and preserving the abbey, and reinstating the heritage orchards and gardens.

Lindores Abbey has authentically recreated an original recipe as a botanical spirit called Aqua Vitae and 2020 saw the release of the first

▲ ***Lindores distillery seen from the historic Lindores Abbey.*** (© Lindores Abbey)

Lindores Abbey single malt whisky in over 500 years. It has won major awards worldwide, including a double gold in the World Spirits Competition. Lindores is a Lowland distillery, although the dividing line between Highland and Lowland distilleries actually runs through the abbey ruins.

Lindores is recognised as the spiritual home of Scotch whisky. In 1494, an Exchequer Roll made the first ever written reference to Scotch whisky. Friar John Cor, a Tironensian monk at Lindores Abbey, was commissioned to turn eight bolls of malt into *aqua vitae*. The Tironensian order were renowned

▲ ***The apothecary's table at Lindores distillery.*** (© Lindores)

for their horticultural skills and were known for their brewing and distilling. A wealthy medieval abbey, Lindores entertained monarchs such as Edward I of England and David II of Scotland. The abbey was destroyed during the Reformation.

Distillery tours are available exploring how whisky is distilled. Participants can try two drams. Sample takeaways are provided for drivers. Well behaved dogs are allowed to accompany their owners on the tours.

The range of activities includes apothecary experiences such as making your own unique *aqua vitae* by blending a range of tinctures, herbs, spices and fruits. Chocolate and whisky pairing sessions are also offered along with tours and whisky flight tasting sessions. Special events are often held, such as bar nights and a Christmas market. There is a shop on site.

All tours should be booked in advance.

Other distilleries in Fife: Darnley's Gin, Eden Mill, Inchdairnie, Kingsbarn, Tayport

LINLITHGOW
Unit 15
Little Mill Business Park
Mill Road Industrial Estate
Linlithgow
Lothian
EH49 7DA
www.linlithgowdistillery.co.uk

Located in Linlithgow, West Lothian, Linlithgow distillery stresses its links with the town's heritage, especially the links with Mary Queen of Scots. Distillation began at Linlithgow in January 2018, and since then it has won numerous awards worldwide.

The Renaissance-style Linlithgow Palace was built in the fifteenth and sixteenth centuries, and was a principal residence of the Scottish monarchs. Mary Queen of Scots was born at the palace in 1542, and lived there for a short time as a child before being sent to France to marry the dauphin, heir to the French Crown. As an adult, she returned to the palace on several occasions including holding her coronation feast at Linlithgow.

▲ ***Interior of Linlithgow distillery.*** (© Linlithgow)

These historic links are reflected in the distillery's bottle design and the flavour profiles depicting the personalities of historical characters. The distillery says that its bottle design features elements from the following iconic buildings in the area:

- the palace, with its horizontal ribbing signifying layers of stone and brick
- St Michael's spire, represented by the bottle's shape and the impression of the crown of thorns spire when viewing the bottle from the top, and in the company logo
- St Magdalene's distillery – the last whisky distillery in Linlithgow, which closed its doors in 1983, is represented by the cupola top to the bottle
- the Maltings – the original malting house for St Magdalene's distillery is also featured in the cupola design
- Linlithgow Loch is represented by the jade green colour of the bottle.

The distillery uses a distillation process known as the maceration technique, in which all the botanicals are present in the mix at all times during the distillation process. There are two stills – this enables the company to reclaim all the 'heads' and 'tails' from each distillation. Only natural flavourings are used. The gin range includes a London dry gin and a berry gin plus limited editions such as the Christmas Mulled Wine gin flavoured with lemon peel, ginger, allspice and cloves. Meadowsweet is a key botanical, and is foraged from the local area. Range extensions include the LinGin colours made after lockdown, aiming to bring fun back into people's lives, and the Four Marys range, inspired by the four ladies in waiting, all of whom were named Mary, who served Mary Queen of Scots. Each of the expressions in the Four Marys is designed to reflect the character and role of the Mary after whom it is named, plus the taste and flavour. A luxury quadruple distilled vodka is produced using the heads and tails from the gin distilling process.

The on-site shop is open between Tuesday to Friday each week. There is a selection of activities that must be pre-booked. The 'Distillery Tour 'n' Tasting' involves exploring the distillery, discovering how LinGin and the Four Marys are created plus a tasting session. Drivers can receive samples to try at home. The 'LinGin Canal Cruise' involves cruising along the Union Canal as far as the Avon Aqueduct while learning about the distillery and tasting gins. The 'Forth Valley Gin Train' is a joint venture between the distillery and the heritage railway. Participants can book places on round trip to Manuel, while discovering the story of Linlithgow gin and trying some of the various ranges, while enjoying hot and cold canapés.

The LinGin canal cruise and the gin train are only available on selected dates – check the website for more details.

Other distilleries in Lothian: Blackness Bay, Glenkinchie, NB Distillery, Secret Garden

LOCH LOMOND
Lomond Estate
Alexandria
West Dumbartonshire
GB3 0TL
www.lochlomandwhiskies.com

Whisky distilling is known to have taken place beside Loch Lomond in 1814. No one knows when it closed but the current distillery started in 1966 when the Glasgow-based Littlemill Distilling Company established a Loch Lomond distillery using straight-neck pot stills. The Bulloch family purchased the distillery in 1985 and steadily developed the business, adding in swan-neck pot stills and continuous stills. It is the only Scottish distillery to have malt and grain production. In 2014, it was taken over by the Loch Lomond Group which increased capacity by adding a third pair of straight-neck stills.

There is an onsite whisky shop offering a full range of Loch Lomond single malt, single grain and limited edition whiskies.

MOFFAT
Dark Sky Spirits
Moffat
Dumfries
DG10 9FE
www.moffatdistillery.com
www.darkskyspirits.com

The Moffat distillery produces hand-crafted small-batch whisky and gin on the only wood-fired stills in Scotland. Dark Sky Spirits was founded in 2017 as a whisky blending company and began the search for a distillery site in 2019. Work began on the site in 2021 and the distillery incorporates a flexible visitor centre allowing a variety of uses including whisky blending workshops and music gigs. Products include the Original Moffat Wood Fired gin, the Local Dram range of blended malt Scotch, including the Doohamer, and a range of Moffat liqueurs. Collaboration with various local charities has resulted in products such as Moffat Mountain Rescue gin and Moffat Eagle Festival and Stranraer Oyster Festival blended malt Scotch whiskies.

Visitors are welcome to visit, enjoy refreshments, whiskies, gins and fruit whisky liqueurs in the Moffat distillery bar. Tours of the distillery combined

The Moffat Distillery, Dark Sky Spirits. (© Moffat)

with a tasting session can be booked in advance via the website.

Other distilleries in Dumfries: Annadale, Bladnoch, Crafty, Dark Art

NB
Halflandbarns
North Berwick
East Lothian
EH39 5PW
www.nbdistillery.com

Located in a coastal town in eastern Scotland beside Tantallon Castle, NB distillery is an independently-owned company. NB stands for the name of the town – North Berwick. Founded in a kitchen 'ginnery' in 2013 and now under new ownership, it has grown steadily. It occupies a purpose-built distillery and operates on an environmentally friendly basis. The distillery has a unique Caribbean-style double retort rum still and a custom-built gin still called 'Gloria'.

It produces a range of award-winning gins and rums, including a low alcohol gin called School Night. NB London dry gin was selected by the royal family on two momentous occasions, chosen by Rolls-Royce as a preferred luxury brand and has been served at the Brit Awards as well as being voted the world's best London dry gin.

NB distillery says it offers a unique experience in which visitors can 'learn, sample and relax' on the five-

▲ ***'Gloria', the gin still at the NB distillery.*** (© NB)

star 'Ginspiration' tours, which are run Tuesday to Saturday each week. These tours must be pre-booked. A gin and tonic accompanies the initial talk about the company's foundation and successes, followed by a tour of the distillery and explanation of gin and rum production methods. The tour ends in the tasting lounge with a guided tasting of a flight of four drinks.

Other distilleries in Lothian: Blackness Bay, Glenkinchie, Linlithgow, Secret Garden

OLD POISON
The Biscuit Factory
Edinburgh
EH6 5NP
www.oldpoison.co.uk

A small craft distillery founded by mixologist Fabrizio Gioffi, Old Poison specialises in creating unique flavours combining traditional and modern distillation processes using herbs, fruits and spices. Typical examples include Distilled Negroni, Hina Cold Brew coffee rum and Bitter Aperitivo.

The unusual distillery name is believed to reflect the ancient medicinal uses of juniper which may, or may not, have been successful. It gives a dark image to the brand, reflected in the labels, which feature pictures of skulls and even a venomous snake curling around a bottle.

Pre-booked tours are available, which include exploring the varied distillation and production techniques, and tasting the full range of seven spirits. Tales are also told of the stories behind the spirits, such as the elder gin, Vesuvius.

Other distilleries and related attractions in Edinburgh: 56 North, Eden Mill, Edinburgh Gin, Holyrood, Johnnie Walker, Lind & Lime, One Square, Port of Leith, Summerhall/ Pickering's Gin, The Scotch Whisky Experience

ONE SQUARE
One Square
1 Festival Square
Edinburgh
EH3 9SR
www.onesquareedinburgh.co.uk

Located close to Edinburgh Castle, One Square is a gin bar and brasserie focusing on seasonal Scottish produce. The gin terrace offers stunning views of the castle. Working with Pickering's, it now offers its own One Square gin, containing a mix of fifteen botanicals.

There is a gin tasting experience which can be booked, providing an insight into the processes of gin distillation, and a seasonal gin tasting combined with paired canapés.

Other distilleries and related attractions in Edinburgh: 56 North, Eden Mill, Edinburgh Gin, Holyrood, Johnnie Walker, Lind & Lime, Old Poison, Port of Leith, Summerhall/Pickering's Gin, The Scotch Whisky Experience

PORT OF LEITH
11 Whisky Quay
Leith
Edinburgh
EH6 6FH
www.leithdistillery.com

The distillery's origins lie in a research programme exploring yeast and fermentation in the production of Scotch whisky which was undertaken by the founders with the International Centre for Brewing and Distilling (ICBD) at Edinburgh's Heriot-Watt University.

Port of Leith distillery is located in an area which for centuries was lined with bonded warehouses where Scotch whisky was matured, blended and bottled. It has developed a new building, the first vertical distillery in Scotland. Grain milling and mashing is located at the top of the building, passing down through fermentation to distillation at the bottom. Production in the building began in January 2024.

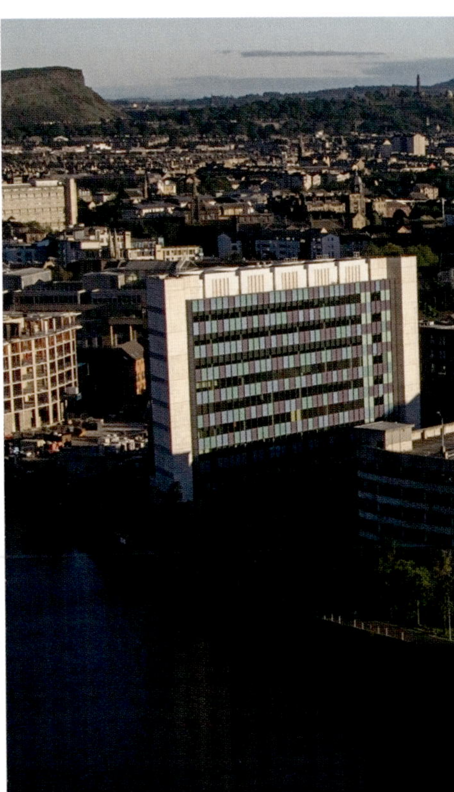

The building is sited on the waterfront itself, and is close to the Ocean Terminal and the royal yacht *Britannia*. The company states that it is now offering a unique experience for visitors, allowing them to get as close to production as possible. It aims to welcome tens of thousands of visitors to the distillery, shop and bar plus flexible spaces being used for exhibitions and public events.

Pre-booked tours are available to explore production at the distillery, and enjoy a tasting of its new-make spirits, port, sherry and guest whisky. Visitors can explore the world's tallest distillery and fill a miniature bottle of new-make spirit. The bar is open daily for drinks and meals Tuesday to Sunday, and tables have to be reserved.

Other distilleries and related attractions in Edinburgh: 56 North, Eden Mill, Edinburgh Gin, Holyrood, Johnnie Walker, Lind & Lime, Old Poison, One Square, Summerhall/ Pickering's Gin, The Scotch Whisky Experience

Port of Leith distillery. (© Port of Leith)

ROSEBANK
Camelon Road
Falkirk
Stirlingshire
FK1 5JR
www.rosebank.com

Local wine merchant James Rankine began distilling on the site in 1840. The result was highly sought after by blenders. It became revered as the 'King of the Lowlands'. Distilling continued until the 1990s when owners UDV (now Diageo) mothballed it. The site was sold to British Waterways, and the original stills and mash tun were stolen over the Christmas/New Year in 2008/2009. Ian Macleod Distillers acquired the site in 2017, with the aim of reviving distilling as well as providing tourist facilities. Over the next few years, the building was steadily restored, and new distilling equipment introduced.

Rosebank produces non-peated, triple distilled Lowland single malt whisky. It is one of the few Scottish distilleries (such as Ardnahoe) that use worm tub condensers, giving a heavier style to the resulting beverage.

Rosebank welcomes visitors and offers a variety of tours which can be booked. These include the 'Rosebank ReAwakening' tour involving a guided tour and the opportunity to taste twelve-year-old whiskies and nose new spirit fresh from the still. The 'Rosebank

Rosebank Distillery. (© Rosebank)

▲ ***Distilling underway at Rosebank distillery.*** (© Rosebank)

Rekindled' tour offers tutored tasting of thirty-one- and fifteen-year-old spirits together with a distillery tour, while 'Rosebank Revered' is a lengthy guided tour, including an introduction to the distillery's meticulous restoration, a look at new-make spirits and an exclusive tasting of rare and Rosebank whiskies. There is a distillery shop on site selling Rosebank products and related locally produced merchandise.

The visitor centre is open seven days a week all year round. Pre-booking is essential for all tours and experiences.

Other distilleries in the area: Falkirk, Stirling

SECRET GARDEN
32A Old Pentland Road
Damhead
Lothianburn
Edinburgh
EH10 7EA
www.secretgardendistillery.co.uk

At the heart of this distillery is an organic 'secret garden' founded on a derelict plot in 2017. It is now home to over 600 varieties of plants harvested for gin-making. As far as possible, everything is used from 'seed to sip'. Two copper stills are used to distil the spirits, and harmonised with botanical flavours showcasing the flavours and

▲ ***Wild gin from the Secret Garden distillery.***
(© Secret Garden)

colours available from nature. The company is family-owned and uses sustainable practices throughout its production and processes.

Secret Garden creates a wide range of gins including unusual ones such as lemon verbena, elderflower and jasmine, lavender or wild organic gin, all made using 100% natural ingredients.

Pre-booked tours are available exploring how the unique gin flavours are created, and sampling some of the gins. The on-site shop offers an opportunity to buy local produce as well as Secret Garden products.

Other distilleries in Lothian: Blackness Bay, Glenkinchie, NB Distillery, Linlithgow

STIRLING
The Old Smiddy
9 Lower Castlehill
Stirling
FK8 1EN
www.stirlingdistillery.com

Launched in 2015, this is a family business. It initially started with the distillation of small-batch craft gin, before expanding into whisky with the launch of a 'Sons of Scotland' independent bottling range. Production of new-make whisky began in 2023, marking the first time whisky has been produced in Stirling since 1852. The first Stirling distillery whisky will be available in 2027. All products are distilled, bottled and labelled on site.

The distillery at Stirling. (© Stirling Distillery)

The distillery is located in an iconic historic building in the shadow of Stirling Castle. According to local legend it was the site of a stables used by King James VI in the 1500s, and the existing building was originally a church temperance hall.

Stirling distillery has its own visitor centre, shop and garden. It offers gin tours, tastings and cocktail masterclasses as well as a gin school enabling visitors to create bespoke gin. All these activities need to be pre-booked. Stirling distillery also operates a variety of one-off events throughout the year.

Other distilleries in Stirlingshire: Falkirk, Rosebank

SUMMERHALL
1 Summerhall
Newington
Edinburgh
EH9 1PL
www.summerhalldistillery.com
www.pickeringsgin.com

Best known for its Pickering's gin brand, Summerhall was the first exclusive gin distillery to be opened in Edinburgh for over 150 years. Located in the premises of the former Royal Dick Vet School, the business was launched in 2013. Owned by two friends who have a background in engineering, furniture restoration and property renovation, the business has developed a reputation for being different. They decided to open a gin distillery simply because they liked gin, and had just inherited a recipe dating back to 1947. They converted the building themselves and built a distillery, while testing and experimenting until they had tailored the 1947 recipe to modern tastes. The original recipe was based on a Bombay recipe redolent of fragrant spices and citrus fruits, but needed adjusting to create a smoother, softer type of gin. To achieve this they devised a special bain-marie heating system for the 500-litre copper stills, thus enabling the botanicals to experience a luxurious simmer during distillation.

Summerhall now produces 2,500 litres of spirit each week and often has unusual combinations such as Brussels Sprout gin and Forget-me-not gin. Apart from its own brand, it has undertaken partnerships with organisations such as the Royal Edinburgh Military Tattoo, Cunard Cruiselines, the Royal Navy and the royal yacht *Britannia*. The company has launched several promotional firsts such as the Pickering's gin 'Baubles', leading to the sale of 30,000 units in 82 seconds.

In 2022, Summerhall expanded into distilling whisky and creating The Broody Hen blended whisky, matured in oak-aged casks sourced from elsewhere in Scotland.

Distillery tours can be pre-booked. Sessions vary in length focusing on different aspects of Pickering's gin and The Broody Hen Scotch whisky experiences including guided tastings sessions. There are also tours focusing on 'Roaring Twenties' gin cocktails and a 'Speakeasy' experience. Tours can be booked between Thursday and Sunday every week.

Other distilleries and related attractions in Edinburgh: 56 North, Eden Mill, Edinburgh gin, Holyrood, Johnnie Walker, Lind & Lime, Old Poison, One Square, Port of Leith, The Scotch Whisky Experience

TAYPORT
Unit 2, Shanwell Court Industrial Estate
Tayport
Fife
DD6 9DX
www.taportdistillery.com

Tayport is a family-owned distillery using only local farm produce to produce its liqueurs, gins and vodkas. Its first spirit was Eau de Vie aperitif, followed by blackcurrant and raspberry liqueurs before launching into gin distilling. Wild Rose was Tayport's first gin, having a London dry style with floral notes, followed by Scots Pine, which has spicier, warmer flavours. The bottle labels show the local landmark, Larick Beacon, reflecting the company's local links.

Tayport distillery offers a distillery tour and cocktail masterclasses. Pre-booking is essential. The tour starts with a discussion of how Tayport began as a family business, how it has developed and how the spirits are distilled, followed by a sampling session. Visitors can take away a miniature that they have personally waxed. The company has an on-site shop selling its spirits and associated merchandise. Tours are held between March and October.

Other distilleries in Fife: Darnley's gin, Eden Mill, Inchdairnie, Kingsbarn, Lindores

THE SCOTCH WHISKY EXPERIENCE
354 Castlehill
Edinburgh EH1 2NE
www.scotchwhiskyexperience.co.uk

Located at the top of the Royal Mile near Edinburgh Castle, The Scotch Whisky Experience is a leisure attraction designed to inspire and educate visitors about Scotch whisky. It offers a guided tour exploring the history and production of Scotch whisky and how whisky differs around the world.

Visitors can book various tours such as 'Tasting Tales' (an hour-long tutored tasting of Scotch whisky with canapés) and 'A Taste of Scotland' (a whisky tour plus a three-course tasting menu in the restaurant). Special events include samplings from various distillers such as Speyside and Morrison. There are also day-long whisky training school sessions resulting in the granting of a certificate of expertise, recognised in the Scotch whisky industry, to each successful participant.

The complex includes the unique Diageo Claive Vidiz whisky collection of 3,384 bottles of whisky, including many rare examples. It forms a snapshot of thirty-five years of Scotch whisky production, and includes many unusual bottlings such as Scottie dogs, monks, golf bags, a seal and an eagle. Every visitor passing through The Scotch Whisky Experience has the opportunity to view this superb collection. Visitors can book a special whisky tasting or dining experience surrounded by the collection.

There is an onsite shop and restaurant.

The Scotch Whisky Experience with Edinburgh Castle in the background.
(© The Scotch Whisky Experience)

Other distilleries and related attractions in Edinburgh: 56 North, Eden Mill, Edinburgh Gin, Holyrood, Johnnie Walker, Lind & Lime, Old Poison, One Square, Port of Leith, Summerhall/ Pickering's Gin

WEE FARM
Forth Mains Farm
Climpy Road,
Forth
South Lanarkshire
ML11 8EN
www.theweefarmdistillery.co.uk

Wee Farm is a micro-distillery set up at a family-owned livestock farm in 2018. It uses a craft copper still named 'Morag II' to double distil traditional botanicals with a native twist. All the small-batch gin is bottled and labelled on the farm. Typical gins include the Drover's, celebrating Scottish agricultural heritage and combining a balance of citrus, thistle, heather, pink peppercorn and allspice botanicals, and the Clydesdale gin, which is designed to celebrate the Clydesdale horse, with flavours of rhubarb and apples. Wee Farm also produces unique gin liqueurs.

The onsite farm shop sells a range of Wee Farm produce including Caledonian Moonshine apple brandy. There are two cottages that can be booked as holiday accommodation. A range of pre-booked activities are available including gin tasting, as well as farm events such as 'Meet the Alpacas'.

Other distilleries in Lanarkshire: Biggar

SPEYSIDE

ABERLOUR
High Street
Aberlour
Banffshire
AB38 9PJ
www.maltwhiskydistilleriess.com/ aberlour

Owned by Pernod-Ricard, Aberlour is a small distillery set on the banks of the River Spey. Founded in 1879 by James Fleming, it uses local spring water flowing over the pink granite of Ben Rinnes to provide the water for making Aberlour whisky. A traditional whisky, Aberlour is double-cask matured in Oloroso sherry and American oak barrels to create a complex Speyside single malt. All the barley used in the production of Aberlour whisky is grown within fifteen miles of the distillery.

Tasting experiences and express flights are available at Aberlour and include tutored nosings of varying types of whisky including rare examples. Other experiences available include an opportunity to meet the alpacas and lambs.

There is no parking on site, and visitors are requested to park in the village and walk to the distillery. Booking in advance is required. The distillery is only open on Friday and Saturdays – access at any other time is by appointment only.

Other distilleries in Banffshire: Ballindalloch, Balvenie, Cardhu, Cragganmore, Glenallchie, Glenfarclas, Glenfiddich, Glen Grant, Glenlivet, Glenrinnes, Speyburn, Speyside Cooperage, Strathisla, Tamnavulin, The Macallan, Tomintoul

BALLINDALLOCH
Ballindalloch
Banffshire
AB37 9AA
www.ballindallochdistillery.com

Work on constructing the Ballindalloch distillery began in 2011, basing it in an old farmstead on the estate dating back to 1848. This is a craft distillery, using produce such as barley grown on the estate that is fed back to cattle afterwards. Whisky distilling has taken place on the estate in the past, such as at the Glenfarclas and Craggenmore distilleries during the nineteenth century. Ballindoch produce single estate whisky, hand-crafted in small batches.

There is an on-site shop open Monday to Friday. Tours and tastings sessions are available, but must be pre-booked. These include guided tours of the distillery. An unusual experience is the hands-on opportunity to take part in the full range of traditional distillery activities from milling to bottling. There is no automation involved, so this day-long experience can be very hard work!

Other distilleries in county: Aberlour, Balvenie, Cardhu, Cragganmore, Glenallchie, Glenfarclas, Glenfiddich, Glen Grant, Glenlivet, Glenrinnes, Speyburn, Speyside Cooperage, Strathisla, Tamnavulin, The Macallan, Tomintoul

BALVENIE
Dufftown
Keith
Banffshire
AB55 4BB
www.thebalvenie.com

Balvenie distillery has been owned by William Grant & Sons since its foundation in 1892, with production starting the following year. The site includes traditional floor maltings, one of the few that remain in use in Scotland. Balvenie uses fresh water from the River Fiddich in the production of its whisky. A wide range of peated whisky is created here. Some are finished in ex-Caroni rum casks, others in American oak casks. The core range gains its specific character from a proprietary process first introduced in 1983 using maturation in two different cask types.

Pre-booked tours of the distillery are available offering an opportunity to experience a guided visit around the different buildings on the distillery site such as the maltings, the distillation area, the cooperage and the warehouse with its countless barrels of maturing whisky. Along the way, visitors meet the various specialists involved in the production process such as the coppersmith, farmer and maltmen. After the tour, visitors enjoy a tasting session of some of the different whiskies produced on site. Balvenie has its own gift shop selling a range of merchandise which is open to any visitor during trading hours.

Other distilleries in Banffshire: Aberlour, Ballindalloch, Cardhu, Cragganmore, Glenallchie, Glenfarclas, Glenfiddich, Glen Grant, Glenlivet, Glenrinnes,, Speyburn, Speyside Cooperage, Strathisla, Tamnavulin, The Macallan, Tomintoul

BENRIACH
Elgin
Moray
IV30 8IH
www.benriachdistillery.com

Founded in 1898 by John Duff, Benriach has had a difficult history. Just two years after construction, the Pattison Crash occurred in which Benriach, like many other distilleries, closed its doors, unable to trade due to the sheer amount of money owed by Glasgow blenders. Benriach remained closed for sixty-five years until its purchase by Glenlivet in 1965. Distillation recommenced on site in that year. Further change came in 1979, when Glenlivet's parent company Seagram decided to use Benriach to produce a peated malt for use in their blends. The first official bottling of a single malt took place in 1994. When Pernod Ricard

Benriach distillery and warehouse. (© Benriach)

acquired Seagram in 2001, production at Benriach decreased, finally being placed in mothballs a year later. In 2004, it was sold to an independent consortium led by Billy Walker. Production quickly recommenced and a new range of peated, single malts was created resulting in a range described as dynamic and exciting.

The Benriach distillery is located in North Speyside. Three distinct styles of single malt whisky are produced on the site: classic unpeated, Highland peated and triple distilled. Water for whisky production is drawn from an underground, mineral-rich aquifer.

A range of experiences can be booked including a guided tour, tasting sessions and 'Grape to Grain', which explores the barrels and casks used to mature the whisky. Special events are held occasionally such as evening experiences celebrating a specific decade, or a deconstructed tasting of various ranges. There is a distillery shop containing a selection Benriach produce.

Other distilleries in Moray: Benromach, Cairn, Cairngorm Gin, Caorunn, Dallas Dhu, Dunphail, Glen Grant, Glen Moray, Red Door Gin

▲ ***Benriach's Rachel Barrie, Brown-Forman master blender, at work.*** (© Benriach)

BENROMACH
Benromach Distillery Company Ltd
Invererne Road
Forres
Moray
IV36 3EB
www.benromach.com
www.reddoorgin.com

Built in 1898 in Forres, near Elgin, the distillery was acquired by the Urquhart family in 1993. It is now operated as a family-owned distillery trading as Gordon & MacPhail. The company also own The Cairn. Benromach has revived a 100-year-old lost Speyside style in which maltings topped up their fires with cuts of peat when coal ran low. Changes in modern-day distilling have meant that this process is often not used, but Benromach has reintroduced this type of drying to create a subtly smoky character, enhancing the flavour profile of its organic whiskies. The production process uses local barley and soft water rising from the Chapelton Spring in the nearby Romach Hills. Whisky ranges on offer include signature produce as well as a limited edition 'Contrast' range, each showcasing new processes, barley type or casks so as to provide something new each time. Flavours involve sweetness, spice and smoke as well as touches of tropical fruits, rich fruits and citrus with aromas of rich sherry and spice leading to dark chocolate.

Benromach distillery. (Dan Prince Benromach)

Benromach also produces Red Door Highland gin, with notes of sea buckthorn, pearls of heather and rowan berries plus seasonal variations such as winter botanicals.

Tours of the distillery are available Monday to Friday, all year round, and must be booked in advance. They includes classic tours exploring history, heritage and production methods, an immersive tour complete with a guided tasting of the Contrast range, a heritage tour and a manager's experience. Special tasting flights are provided to experience all the whiskies. For gin lovers, there is a Red Door Gin visitor experience linked in to hand-crafted Highland gins.

Other distilleries in Moray: Benriach, Cairn, Cairngorm gin, Caorunn, Dallas Dhu, Dunphail, Glen Moray, Red Door Gin

CAIRN
Craggan
Grantown-on-Spey
Moray
PH26 3NT
www.thecairndistillery.com

A modern distillery located in the Cairngorms National Park, Cairn is owned by Gordon & MacPhail, a fourth-generation family business that initially began as nineteenth-century retailers. Over the years, the company has expanded to become wholesalers, whisky bottlers and distillery owners. It remains a family business. Described as a progressive distillery, it is designed to maximise flavour and character and produce outstanding whiskies. The first whiskies distilled at Cairn will be released in the 2030s but visitors are able to enjoy a range of unique sherry cask matured, unpeated expressions.

Various guided tours are available and must be pre-booked. These include an 'Explorer' tour focusing on how the local environment inspires Cairn's approach to Scotch whisky as well as distillery tours and tasting sessions. There is a shop on site, as well as a range of outdoor trails along the banks of the River Spey to explore. 'The Gathering' is a licensed café offering a wide range of food including tapas. Opening hours are Tuesday to Saturday.

Other distilleries in Moray: Benriach, Benromach, Cairngorm, Caorunn, Dallas Dhu, Dunphail, Glen Moray, Red Door Gin

CAIRNGORM GIN
Unit 4
Granish Industrial Park,
Aviemore
PH22 1QD
www.cairngormgin.com

Cairngorm was founded in 2019 and describes itself as a progressive, Scottish micro-distillery. Spirits are distilled in small batches using water from the River Spey and its first release was a signature edition Cairngorm gin inspired by the locality.

The stills at Cairngorm Gin. (© Cairngorm Gin)

The distillery and shop is fully open to the public and can be visited between Tuesday and Saturday all year round. Booking in advance is recommended. Visitors can see where Cairngorm's range of artisan craft gins are produced, and buy produce in the shop. Also stocked in store are ranges of locally produced seasonal merchandise. Visitors can try sample bottles of Cairngorm gin. Cairngorm is dog friendly as long as dogs are kept on leads.

Other distilleries in Moray: Benriach, Benromach, Cairn, Caorunn, Dallas Dhu, Dunphail, Glen Moray, Red Door Gin

CAORUNN
Balmenach Distillery
Cromdale
Balmenach Road
Grantown-on-Spey
Moray
PH26 3PF
www.caorunngin.com

The name Caorunn is inspired by the Gaelic word for rowan berry, one of the botanicals used in the creation of the Caorunn gin. The distillery is the only one in the world to create hand-crafted small-batch gin using a copper berry chamber to extract maximum

Caorunn Distillery. (© Caorunn)

flavour. It now produces a range of gins including Blood Orange and Chilli, and an aged version that has been matured in Spanish oak casks. An unusual range is the Highland strength gin which is bottled at a higher alcohol strength (54% ABV). It is essentially the same as the classic gin, but with less water added during bottling, so it has a more concentrated flavour.

Balmenach is also a malt whisky distillery, with the resultant whisky being used almost entirely in blended whisky. It was licensed to produce Scotch whisky in 1824. There are no tours of the whisky distillery available. Balmenach and Caorunn are owned by International Beverages, which is in turn owned by Thai Bev. International Beverages also owns the Speyburn, Knockdhu, Balblair and Pulteney distilleries.

The visitor centre focuses on Caorunn gin production. It is open five days a week, closed at weekends. A guided tour can be booked, exploring the copper berry chamber distillation process, how gin is distilled and the botanicals used, followed by a tutored nosing and tasting sessions. There is a shop on site.

Other distilleries in Moray: Benriach, Benromach, Cairn, Cairngorm gin, Dallas Dhu, Dunphail, Glen Moray, Red Door Gin

CARDHU
Knockando
Aberlour
Banffshire
AB38 7RW
www.malts.com/en-row/distilleries/cardhu

Founded by whisky smuggler John Cumming and his wife Helen in 1824, Cardhu distillery later passed into the control of their daughter Elizabeth. According to local tradition, Helen used to disguise the smell of whisky by claiming she was baking bread and offer the Excise officers a cup of tea. While they were drinking it, she would fly a flag outside to alert other illegal distilleries to their presence.

Cardhu was the first distillery to partner with John Walker & Sons over 200 years ago. It is now part of the Diageo group. Apart from providing malt whisky for the Johnnie Walker blend, Cardhu produces peaty single malt Scotch whisky which is described as having a sweet, mellow style reflecting the peat-softened waters of the Mannoch Hills.

Distillery tours are available, and should be booked in advance. These include the 'Immersive Journey' tour with a tutored tasting, the 'Collection' tour, and a 'Guess Dhu' tasting experience. Although the tours are available all year, they may be cancelled at short notice due to weather conditions during the winter.

Cardhu also has a bar, known as the Tasting Kitchen, where visitors can enjoy a drink, coffee and sharing platters. Extra behind the scenes tours and activities are available during the annual Spirit of Speyside Festival.

Other distilleries in Banffshire: Aberlour, Ballindalloch, Balvenie, Cragganmore, Glenallchie, Glenfarclas, Glenfiddich, Glen Grant, Glenlivet, Speyburn, Speyside Cooperage, Strathisla, Tamnavulin, The Macallan, Tomintoul

CRAGGANMORE
Ballindalloch
Banffshire
AB37 9AB
www.malts.com/en-row/distilleries/cragganmore

Sister distillery to Cardhu, Cragganmore is located just fifteen minutes away by car. It was founded in 1869 by John Smith, who had earlier been involved in other distilleries such as Glenlivet and The Macallan. The location was carefully chosen to take advantage of the nearby Strathspey Railway, resulting in the first 'whisky special' containing 300 casks of Craggonmore whisky leaving the area in 1887. It now owned by Diageo and is one of the smallest distilleries in the area. Cragganmore distillery has been described as producing the most complex Strathspey single malt. Much of its production is used for blending, but it now offers a range of single malts. All the water used in the distillery comes from the adjacent mineral-rich Craggan Burn. All distillation takes place in iconic pot stills possessing a flat top and short neck, helping to create the distinctive taste. Maturation takes place in sherry, bourbon and port wine casks.

Pre-booked tours are available between March and October. These include guided tours of the distillery, tutored tastings and a warehouse tasting experience. There is a gift shop and café on site.

Other distilleries in Banffshire: Aberlour, Ballindalloch, Balvenie, Cardhu, Glenallchie, Glenfarclas, Glenfiddich, Glen Grant, Glenlivet, , Speyburn, Speyside Cooperage, Strathisla, Tamnavulin, The Macallan, Tomintoul

DALLAS DHU
Mannchie Road
Forres
Moray
IV36 2RR
www.historicenvironment.scot/visit-a-place/places/dallas-dhu

At Dallas Dhu historic distillery it is possible to step back in time to discover how the Roderick Dhu blend of malt whisky was made in the 1900s. Production ceased in 1983, and the distillery passed into the care of Historic Environment Scotland. All the traditional distilling equipment can be seen just as it was in the early 1980s. Since the 1990s it has been a visitor attraction exploring the history of whisky in the area and offering insights into traditional production methods. Plans have been announced by Historic Environment Scotland to restart the site as a working distillery showcasing artisanal methods and how they reflect the history of Speyside whisky. The refurbishment is managed by Aceo Distillers.

The new visitor centre and museum space will provide tours focusing on Scotch whisky and Speyside production of the same. Among the plans for the site include are a virtual reality whisky experience exploring the science behind whisky, the economic story of Speyside whisky, a cooperage display and a café/restaurant.

Other distilleries in Moray: Benriach, Benromach, Cairn, Cairngorm Gin, Caorunn, Dunphail, Glen Moray, Red Door Gin

DUNPHAIL
Wester Greens
Dunphail
Forres
Moray
IV36 2QR
www.dunphaildistillery.com

Dunphail is a traditional distillery, producing single malt whisky. It performed its first distillation on

▲ ***Dunphail distillery.*** (© Dunphail)

6 October 2023. All the barley used on site is prepared in a traditional malthouse complete with working kiln and pagoda roof. A refurbished former farm using heritage materials including the original stonework, Dunphail is sited in a rural location. Dunphail single malt is matured in a range of cask types featuring quality sherries as well as small quantities of both ruby and tawny port. While the Dunphail single malt is maturing, Dunphail has created a series of whiskies known as the Dava Way, named after a local walking trail that passes close by.

Guided tours are available throughout the year but have to be pre-booked, and include a tour of the distillery, warehouse and tasting session. The visitor centre is pet friendly, and open Tuesday to Saturday for tours and shop visits. Visitors can take advantage of an exclusive distillery hand-fill facility allowing them to bottle their own whisky straight from the cask. Refreshments are available on site.

Other distilleries in Moray: Ballindalloch, Benriach, Benromach (including Red Door Gin), Cardhu, GlenAllachie, Glen Moray

GLENALLACHIE
Aberlour
Banffshire
AB38 9LR
www.glenallachie.com

Initially owned by Chivas Brothers, whisky production began in 1968. GlenallAchie distilled single malt whisky, which Chivas used as a component in its blended whisky recipes. This practice changed in 2017 when GlenAllachie was acquired by whisky legend Billy Walker and his two business partners. The following year, the first core range single malts was launched. These malts were extremely successful, and the company's portfolio has steadily grown to include MacNairs, White Heather and Meikle Tòir. GlenAllachie's ten-year-old cask strength won the World's Best Single Malt at the World Whisky Awards 2021. The company has recently sought to increase the sustainability of its produce by installing solar panels to power mechanical vapour recompression technology, aiming to halve energy demand on the site.

The visitor centre was launched in 2019 at the Spirit of Speyside Whisky Festival and is now open seven days a week between April and October. During the winter period of November to March the visitor centre is closed on Sundays. A range of guided tours and tastings must be pre-booked. There is a 'Connoisseur' tour of the distillery

The GlenAllachie distillery. (© Glenallachie)

and warehouse, and a tutored 'Exclusive Single Cask' tasting. Visitors have the opportunity to hand-fill a bottle from a cask. Drivers taking part in a tour can opt for sample bottles to enjoy later.

There is a separate whisky bar and tasting lounge containing a wide range of GlenAllachie core and limited range spirits and offering bespoke tasting flights. This area is walk-in, and no bookings are required.

Other distilleries Banffshire: Aberlour, Ballindalloch, Balvenie, Cardhu, Cragganmore, Glenfarclas, Glenfiddich, Glen Grant, Glenlivet, Speyburn, Speyside Cooperage, Strathisla, Tamnavulin, The Macallan, Tomintoul

GLENFARCLAS
Ballindalloc
Banffshire
AB37 9BD
www.glenfarclas.com

The Grants of Glenfarclas have owned the distillery since 1865. It produces a range of traditional Speyside-style, single Highland malts. These include 105 cask strength at 60% volume and an aged selection between ten and forty years old. Flavours and aromas include toffee, sherried sweetness to hints of dark chocolate, raisins and sultanas.

Each year, Glenfarcas hosts the Spirit of Speyside Festival, with a variety of special events such as a traditional Scottish breakfast held in the stillhouse,

Glenfarclas distillery. (© Glenfarclas)

a whisky BBQ and a 1950s tour. It is also the starting point for the annual 'Dramathon' – marathon races of varying distances along the Speyside Way from Glenfarclas to Glenfiddich, each of which requires participants to drink a dram at each distillery along the way.

Glenfarclas has a long history of welcoming visitors to the site, having opened its first visitor centre in 1973. Several guided tours are available on a pre-booked basis. These include a tour of the distillery, the 'Five Decades' tour and tasting focusing on the family cask collection between 1960 and the 2000s. There is a shop selling Glenfarclas merchandise, but there's no café or restaurant.

Other distilleries in Banffshire: Aberlour, Ballindalloch, Balvenie, Cardhu, Cragganmore, Glenallchie, Glenfiddich, Glen Grant, Glenlivet, Speyburn, Speyside Cooperage, Strathisla, Tamnavulin, The Macallan, Tomintoul

GLENFIDDICH
Dufftown
Keith
Banffshire
AB55 4DH
www.glenfiddich.com

Owned by William Grant & Sons, Glenfiddich was founded in Dufftown in 1887. The name is Gaelic for 'valley of the deer'. The distillery was actually hand-built by William Grant and his nine children, with the aid of a stonemason. Coppersmiths are always on site tending to Glenfiddich's uniquely shaped and sized stills. Glenfiddich has had a dedicated cooperage since 1959. Whisky is matured in bourbon and sherry casks.

The site includes the main distillery and warehouse, home to the company's unique solera vat process which creates a complex, intense flavoured fifteen-year-old whisky. Glenfiddich is now the world's most awarded single malt scotch whisky, while in 2011 it released a unique limited expression, known as Janet Sheed Roberts Reserve. The eleven bottles were auctioned for charity and became the most expensive single malt in the world. In 2021, Glenfiddich launched a series of limited edition collectors' whiskies aimed at investors.

Pre-booked tours are available. These include a distillery tour and a solera deconstructed tour, complete with sample tasting and the preparation of a bespoke version for bottling ready to take home. The visitor centre includes a gift shop, tasting area and café. The centre is open Monday to Sunday, with tours available between Wednesday and Sunday.

Other distilleries in Banffshire: Aberlour, Ballindalloch, Balvenie, Cardhu, Cragganmore, Glenallchie, Glenfarclas, Glen Grant, Glenlivet, Speyburn, Speyside Cooperage, Strathisla, Tamnavulin, The Macallan, Tomintoul

GLEN GRANT
Elgin Road
Rothes
Aberlour
Banffshire
AB38 7BS
www.glengrant.com

Established in 1840, by John and James Grant, brothers who had formerly been whisky smugglers, the business was helped by the decision of James Grant to launch the Morayshire Railway Company, operating between the port of Lossiemouth and Elgin. One of the locomotives was named *Glen Grant*. Ownership of the distillery passed to another family member in 1872 who was also named James Grant. Later he became known as the 'Major' and was renowned for his work in revolutionising single malt whisky by using water cooling purifiers and elongated stills to capture vapours, resulting in the colour and malty flavour which continues to characterise Glen Grant's produce. Glen Grant is the only distiller in Speyside to bottle all its whisky on site. Although the Campari Group now owns the distillery, Dennis Malcolm, one of the descendants of the original brothers, remains the master distiller. Glen Grant whisky is gently peated and has a sweet, fruity palate.

A visitor centre was opened in 2008 and there is also a 22-acre Victorian garden area accessible to the public. Pre-booked tours are available including connoisseur experiences, and a distillery tour covering the various production areas such as the copper pot stills and bottling, and the tasting room. The garden was founded in 1886 and forms a global greenhouse reflecting the Major's adventures around the world, including meadows and scenic gorges. An unusual feature is the Major's dram pavilion. The centre is open all year, but closed on Sundays between November and March inclusive.

Other distilleries in Banffshire: Aberlour, Ballindalloch, Balvenie, Cardhu, Cragganmore, Glenallchie, Glenfarclas, Glenfiddich, Glenlivet, Speyburn, Speyside Cooperage, Strathisla, Tamnavulin, The Macallan, Tomintoul

GLENLIVET
Ballindalloch
Banffshire
AB37 9DB
www.theglenlivet.com

Now owned by the Chivas Brothers subsidiary of Pernod Ricard, Glenlivet is one of the most well known Scotch whisky distilleries producing over 6 million bottles every year. Most of this produce is sold as Glenlivet single malt, with the remainder being used for blends elsewhere in the group.

The founder of Glenlivet was George Smith, who set up the first licensed distillery in the area in 1824. He even had to defend it from smugglers, who threatened to burn down his distillery. Undeterred, he continued trading and refused to work with the smugglers. Glenlivet has traded continuously ever since, apart from a short spell during the First World War. Glenlivet eventually became the original Speyside single malt, a smooth and well balanced whisky. Water for the production process comes from springs in the area. Lantern-shaped stills with long, narrow necks are used to distil the spirit, before it is matured in oak casks. Interestingly, barley seeds from Glenlevit were sent to the International Space Station in May 2021 as part of experiments in outer space. On their return to Earth, the seeds were planted and distilled to create a single malt.

Closed Mondays, pre-booked tours are available between Tuesday and Sunday each week. Visitors can choose from a variety of immersive whisky experiences and tutored tastings. The Drawing Room Bar enables visitors to taste whiskies by the dram, try cocktails and enjoy bar snack pairings. Keen walkers can explore one of the three signposted 'Smugglers' Trail' paths across the adjacent countryside.

Other distilleries in Banffshire: Aberlour, Ballindalloch, Balvenie, Cardhu, Cragganmore, Glenallchie, Glenfarclas, Glenfiddich, Glenlivet, Speyburn, Speyside Cooperage, Strathisla, Tamnavulin, The Macallan, Tomintoul

GLEN MORAY
Bruceland Road
Elgin
Moray
IV30 1YE
www.glenmoray.com

The origins of Glen Moray began with a brewery known as Elgin West, which began producing local ales in 1830. In 1897, it began producing whisky made from local barley and matured in varying types of casks such as Marsala wine and sherry. This tradition has continued, with existing single malt whiskies being matured in several different types of casks including Chardonnay and Cabernet Sauvignon, creating a very distinctive aroma and flavour. There is also a classic peated single malt. Apart from a short period during the First World War, Glen Moray has traded continuously and has been steadily expanded, with new warehouses and more copper stills added. By 1987, it was producing 2 million litres of spirit every year. Innovation has continued to characterise Glen Moray whisky with special limited editions such as a Rhum Agricole, finished in casks from Martinique's St James distillery, resulting in whisky that is rich with spices and dark toffee. Glen Moray is owned by the French La Martiniquaise spirits group.

Opening hours vary according to the season. From October to April, the centre is only open weekdays. Between May and the end September opening hours are extended to include Saturdays. It is closed on Sundays. The visitor centre includes a small gift shop and coffee shop, complete with outside seating area. Pre-booking is essential. Visitors can choose from a selection of activities including a heritage tour and a chocolate and whisky tasting session. There is also an immersive tasting opportunity held in Glen Moray House, enabling visitors to explore the company's history. A variety of pre-booked special events such as breakfast tours are held during the annual Spirit of Speyside Festival in May.

Other distilleries in Moray: Benriach, Benromach, Cairn, Cairngorm Gin, Caorunn, Dallas Dhu, Dunphail, Glenfiddich, Red Door Gin

GLENRINNES
Glenrinnes Lodge
Dufftown
Keith
Banffshire
www.glenrinnes.com/distillery

Glennrinnes produces the Eight Lands organic spirits range and organic Speyside gin and vodka. The name is inspired by the eight counties to be seen from Ben Rinnes, a mountain located beside the distillery.

Glenrinnes distillery. (© Glenrinnes)

Glenrinnes offers a range of pre-booked tours including a standard forty-five-minute visitor experience. Driver's packs are available. There are also VIP luxury, immersive tours which involve a guided tour of the estate focusing on organic farming, before heading to the distillery to explore gin production and receive a tutored tasting.

Other distilleries in Banffshire: Aberlour, Ballindalloch, Balvenie, Cardhu, Cragganmore, Glenallchie, Glenfarclas, Glenfiddich, Glen Grant, Glenlivet, Speyburn, Speyside Cooperage, Strathisla, Tamnavulin, The Macallan,Tomintoul

GORDON CASTLE
The Walled Garden
Gordon Castle
Fochabers
Moray
Scotland
www.gordoncastlescotland.com

Gordon Castle runs its own gin school enabling participants to take part in a full distillation course involving a traditional copper pot mini-still. After foraging for botanicals, participants make their own small-batch gin. Pre-booking is essential. Also on offer at Gordon Castle shop are the Gordon Castle gin ranges, including personalised gin with engraved bottles.

Gordon Castle is part of a historic estate. The castle dates back to 1479, and was transformed by the Duke of Gordon in the late eighteenth century to create a grand baronial mansion with a frontage of 568 feet. Gordon Castle has long been involved in the whisky industry. It was the involvement of the Fifth Duke of Gordon that led to the legalisation of Highland whisky distilling, having informed Parliament that his tenants in Strathavon and

Gordon Castle. (© Gordon Castle)

Glenlivet could not be prevented from illicitly distilling whisky so why not allow it and collect the taxes? As soon as the requisite Act of Parliament was passed in 1823, the duke encouraged his tenant George Smith to establish a legal still at Glenlivet, where the distillery still operates today.

Visitors are welcome to explore the Walled Garden, which is one of the oldest and largest kitchen gardens in the UK. There is also a café on site, as well as holiday cottages and luxury accommodation. The castle itself is not open to the public.

Other distilleries in the area: Benriach, Benromach, Cairn, Cairngorm Gin, Caorunn, Dallas Dhu, Dunphail, Glen Moray, Red Door Gin

KINRARA
Lynwilg Farm Steading
Aviemore
PH22 1PZ
www.kinaradistillery.com

The area surrounding the Kinrara gin distillery is known as the Kinrara Estate, and possesses outstanding scenic and nature conservation value, as well as historical interest. Founded in 2017, the distillery is located in a former milking shed from which small-batch production processes blend traditional spirits designed to appeal to modern tastes. The range includes its signature Highland dry plus special editions like Freya the Fox and Ginny the Cow.

Located close to Aviemore, Kinara offers gin tasting experiences, tasting rooms and a distillery shop.

KNOCKDHU
Knock
Huntly
Aberdeenshire
AB54 7LJ
www.ancnoc.com

In 1892, John Morrison acquired the Knock Estate, having noticed an opportunity to create a great whisky, since the area was rich in peat and barley and possessed its own source of pure water springs. These advantages were further aided by the fact that the Great North of Scotland Railway operated nearby. The resultant distillery was built from local grey granite. It traded continuously until 1931 before hitting problems due to economic depression and wartime restrictions. In 1988, it became the first distillery to be acquired by Inver House Distillers and since then it has steadily grown in stature.

Although the distillery is named Knockdhu, the whisky produced here is actually branded anCnoc (a Gaelic word meaning 'the hill'). Whisky is produced in the same style of pot stills used

Knockdhu distillery. (© Knockdhu)

in 1892. These stills have a bulbous base and tall, slender necks creating whisky with a very light, fresh flavour. Knockdhu produces a range of whisky included peated versions that are finished in sherry casks.

There is no visitor centre but Knockdhu offers daily guided tours around the distillery exploring the company's history and production methods. These pre-booked tours take place on weekdays only, between Monday and Friday.

RED DOOR GIN
Benromach Distillery
Invererne Road
Forres
Moray
IV36 3EB
www.reddoorgin.com

Red Door produces small-batch Highland gin infused with juniper and other locally inspired botanicals designed to reflect the spirit of the Highland countryside. There are separate versions to reflect the different seasons. The company uses a hand-made copper pot still.

Pre-booked guided tours of the distillery are available and Red Door is the only distillery in Speyside to offer a single-site gin and whisky visitor experience. There is a shop on site.

Other distilleries in Moray: Benriach, Benromach, Cairn, Dallas Dhu, Dunphail, Glen Moray

SPEYBURN

Rothes
Aberlour
Banffshire
AB38 7AG
www.speyburn.com

Speyburn distillery was founded in 1897 by John Hopkins, a whisky merchant, who wanted to create his own distinctive brand of Scotch whisky. He invited architect Charles C. Doig to design a building that blended into the landscape. This was not an easy task, as it had to be constructed over three levels in order to match the steep topography of the valley. As a result, Doig had to create a very different type of distillery, complete with an iconic pagoda ventilator allowing a constant current of air to flow over the grains.

The use of height to fit Speyburn onto a compact site relates to the drum maltings. When Speyburn was built, the conventional arrangement was for a floor maltings. There simply wasn't space for a floor maltings at Speyburn, which is why the drum maltings design was chosen since it replaces the malting floor with more compact drums. The floor above the drums houses the steeping tanks, with a grain store on the top level. This represented state of the art technology for the period.

Hopkins was a very determined man, and even though the building was not complete insisted on starting the distilling process as quickly as possible in order to produce his first whisky in honour of Queen Victoria's Diamond Jubilee. The drum maltings were not completed until 1905, but they remained in continuous use, with a short break during the Second World War, before finally being mothballed in 1967.

In 1916, Hopkins sold the business to The Distillers Company Ltd which continued production until 1939. The outbreak of war resulted in the distillery being shut down for the duration, to become home to Scottish artillery regiments. By 1962, indirect steam heating had replaced coal-fired stills. Ownership changed again in 1992 when the company became part of Inver House Distillers, leading to production capacity being doubled.

Speyburn is the only distillery in the area to use the fast-flowing mineral rich water of the nearby Granty Burn. The result is a smooth, refreshing whisky.

Variations across the range include the sweeter Bradan Orach and the richer fifteen-year-old Speyburn. Speyburn is not a peated whisky.

Speyburn distillery is located in the picturesque town of Rothes, in the centre of the Speyside Whisky Trail. The visitor centre offers an immersive experience exploring the history and production methods relating to Speyburn whisky. Each guided tour goes behind the scenes enabling visitors to explore the distillery and the old drum maltings, ending with an opportunity to taste the Speyburn range and receive a complimentary Glencairn glass. The centre is open all year, every Tuesday to Saturday. Pre-booking is recommended.

Other distilleries in Banffshire: Aberlour, Ballindalloch, Balvenie, Cardhu, Cragganmore, Glenallchie, Glenfarclas, Glenfiddich, Glen Grant, Glenlivet, Glenrinnes, Speyside Cooperage, Strathisla, Tamnavulin, The Macallan, Tomintoul

SPEYSIDE COOPERAGE
Dufftown Road
Craigellachie
Banffshire
AB38 9SS
www.speysidecooperage.co.uk

Speyside Cooperage is the official world record-holder for the fastest time it takes to craft a 190-litre barrel.

Guided tours must be booked in advance. These tours take place every hour, weekdays only. The tours allow visitors to see how barrels and casks are made by trained coopers, using skills that have taken years to learn, as well as discovering the importance of the relationship between cask and contents. The tour ends with a tasting session of Speyside's own-label ten-year-old single malt.

Other distilleries in Banffshire: Aberlour, Ballindalloch, Balvenie, Cardhu, Cragganmore, Glenallchie, Glenfarclas, Glenfiddich, Glen Grant, Glenlivet, Speyburn, Strathisla, Tamnavulin, The Macallan,Tomintoul

STRATHISLA
Seafield Avenue
Keith
Banffshire
AB55 5BS
www.maltwhiskydistilleries.com/strathisla

This is the spiritual home of Chivas whisky and is the oldest working distillery in the Scottish Highlands, dating back to 1786. A riverside distillery in the town of Keith, it is a short walk from the train station.

Originally, this was the Milltown distillery, founded by George Taylor and Alexander Milne who had leased the land from the Earl of Seafield. Over the next 200 years, ownership changed hands several times, finally being acquired by Chivas.

Chivas had long been involved in the Scotch whisky industry, having been founded by two brothers John and James Chivas who had a luxury grocery shop in Aberdeen. When customers began asking for whisky, they promptly began blending whisky in the shop cellar, setting standards for the art of whisky blending. In 1843, Chivas gained its first royal warrant, providing whisky to Queen Victoria at Balmoral.

Strathisla distillery is open all year round to visitors, although opening hours are slightly shorter in winter. During the guided tours, visitors explore the history of the site and the Chivas brand, learn about production methods and enjoy a guided tasting of Chivas whisky. Various other tours and tasting experiences can be booked such as of the newly renovated No. 3 dunnage warehouse, a Chivas blending workshop, a 'Royal Salute' experience – which includes access to the Royal Salute Vault – as well as a special tour of the vault which contains the most cherished whiskies produced by the Chivas brand. Other facilities on site include a shop.

Other distilleries in Banffshire: Aberlour, Ballindalloch, Balvenie, Cardhu, Cragganmore, Glenallchie, Glenfarclas, Glenfiddich, Glen Grant, Glenlivet, Glenrinnes,Speyburn, Speyside Cooperage, Tamnavulin, The Macallan, Tomintoul

TAMNAVULIN
Tamnavulin
Ballindalloch
Banffshire
AB37 9JA
www.tamnavulinwhisky.com

For much of the year, Tamnavulin is not open to the public. It makes an exception during the annual Spirit of Speyside Festival when it participates in various events.

It was founded in 1966 in a rural village location on the site of an old carding mill. Following a major refurbishment, it reopened in 1995. It produces a range of artisan single malt whisky possessing a sweet, fruity flavour.

Other distilleries in Banffshire: Aberlour, Ballindalloch, Balvenie, Cardhu, Cragganmore, Glenallchie, Glenfarclas, Glenfiddich, Glen Grant, Glenlivet, Glenrinnes,Speyburn, Speyside Cooperage, Strathisla, The Macallan, Tomintoul

THE MACALLAN DISTILLERY EXPERIENCE
The Macallan Distillers Ltd
Easter Elchies
Craigellachie
Banffshire
AB38 9RX
www.themacallan.com

In 1824, Alexander Reid set up The Macallan distillery on the Easter Elchies estate. He had formerly worked as a

▲ ***The origin of Macallan distillers.*** (© Macallan)

teacher and farmer, and was fascinated by the distilling process. From the very beginning of the company, he established core production principles that have never changed. He believed that small stills produce better flavour and character, so avoided using large, high volume stills in favour of small ones to provide high quality whisky.

The company celebrated its two-hundredth anniversary with a special sensory experience involving a month long Cirque Du Soleil SPIRIT experience located at the Macallan Estate. It also introduced a limited edition 1949 vintage whisky bottled in 2022 known as Tales of the Macallan Volume II, accompanied by a bespoke Lalique crystal decanter and an illustrated almanac telling the story of Alexander Reid. Some of the illustrations were used to create a short zoetrope-style animated film.

Over the years, The Macallan has built a global reputation as a leading single malt whisky. It is now a wholly owned subsidiary of the privately owned Edrington spirits company, which also own brands such as Glenrothes and Highland Park.

The name is derived from the Gaelic word *magh*, meaning fertile ground, and 'Ellan', derived from the monk named St Fillan who is linked to a medieval church situated on the estate. It was a local tradition for farmers to make whisky during the winter months from their surplus barley. The Macallan Estate now occupies 485 acres in an area of natural beauty.

▲ ***Toasting casks.*** (© The Macallan)

The distillery possesses twenty-four of the smallest copper stills on Speyside, each capable of holding an initial charge of 3,900 litres. The whisky is matured in oak casks, seasoned with sherry wine from Jerez in Spain. It is these casks which give the whisky its distinctive golden colour. Ranges available include The Macallan's signature classic range including twelve-, eighteen- and thirty-year-old whiskies plus various limited releases of rare single malts such as the James Bond sixtieth anniversary malt.

Opened in 2018, the visitor centre provides a range of experiences including heritage discovery sessions focusing on distillation and sampling, a whisky tasting exploring the impact of oak cask maturation, a flight of The Macallan through the ages and a personal shopping experience. The Macallan Bar provides sampling sessions, while the Elchies Brasserie serves Scottish produce. Sample packs are provided for drivers to take away.

Pre-booking at least twenty-four hours in advance is essential. All visits to The Macallan Estate are by appointment only – this includes the Elchies Brasserie, The Macallan Bar and The Macallan Boutique, which sells a range of The Macallan-related merchandise including tableware and cocktail materials.

The company says it is not safe to walk to the distillery, as there are no pedestrian paths leading to the entrance. The nearest train stations are Aviemore, Keith and Elgin.

Other distilleries in Banffshire: Aberlour, Ballindalloch, Balvenie, Cardhu, Cragganmore, Glenallchie, Glenfarclas, Glenfiddich, Glen Grant, Glenlivet, Glenrinnes, Speyburn, Speyside Cooperage, Tamnavulin, Tomintoul

THE SNUG FROM SPEYSIDE
Aviemore Retail Park
Cairngorms
PH22 1AF
www.thesnugspeysidedistillery.co.uk
www.speysidedistillery.co.uk

The Snug is the visitor centre for Speyside distillery, a private distillery based at the nearby Tromie Mills, Kingussie.

Founded by John and Robert Harvey, the recipe for Speyside whisky was officially written down as the 'Harvey's Codex' in 1856, covering everything from the exact details for malting, the choice of Highland water and the best wood/cask selection. During the 1920s – the American Prohibition era – Spey whisky became a lucrative export to Chicago and New York attracting customers like Al Capone, George Remus and Belle Livingstone. Ownership of the Speyside distillery changed several times over the years, but in 2012 one of the descendants of the original brewing family, John Harvey McDonough, re-acquired the business.

Located in the Cairngorm Mountains, Speyside distillery has been described as one of the prettiest in the area set amid evergreen forests and beside the River Tromie. It has appeared on TV as the fictional Lagganmore from the BBC series *Monarch of the Glen*.

Speyside is now an artisan business, a small family-owned distillery with every aspect of whisky production taking place under one roof. It uses only traditional methods, plus locally sourced barley, brewers' yeast and water from the adjacent River Tomie. The result is a whisky that is distinctively fruity and floral.

The Snug contains a shop selling Speyside merchandise and an art gallery, as well as hosting whisky flight tastings. Guided tours to Speyside distillery can be booked at the Snug and are only available by prior appointment on specific dates.

TOMINTOUL
Ballindalloch
Banffshire
AB37 9AQ
www.tomintoulwhisky.com

Tomintoul distillery was founded in 1965 and is part of Angus Dundee Distillers. Ballindalloch is quite a scenic

Tomintoul from the Air. (© Tomintoul)

location, being the highest village in the Scottish Highlands.

The distillery uses only traditional techniques to create an award-winning single malt whisky, which is matured in American oak ex-bourbon barrels. There are a variety of flavours including peated and cognac cask finish.

Guided tours of the distillery are available, but must be pre-booked. These are only available at set times and days. There are separate

warehouse-only tours. Each tour has only a limited number of places, and operates on a seasonal basis.

Other distilleries in Banffshire: Aberlour, Ballindalloch, Balvenie, Cardhu, Cragganmore, Glenallchie, Glenfarclas, Glenfiddich, Glen Grant, Glenlivet, Glenrinnes,Speyburn, Speyside Cooperage, Strathisla, The Macallan, Tamnavulin

USEFUL RESOURCES

Books

Eyewitness Companion to Whisky, by Charles Maclean
Dorling Kindersley 2008

Scotch Whisky: A Liquid History, by Charles Maclean,
Cassell Illustrated, 2004

The Gin Clan: Scottish Gins and Distilleries, by Fiona Laing,
Great Northern Books 2019

The Weird and Wonderful story of gin, by Angela Youngman
Pen & Sword Books 2022

Whiskey: A Global History, by Kevin R. Kosar
Reaction books Ltd 2010

Whisky: The Manual, by Dave Broom
Mitchell Beazley 2014

Organisations

The Scotch Whisky Association
www.scotch-whisky.org.uk